BLACK & DECKER®

PORTABLE

WORKSHOP

Basic Wood Projects
with Portable Power Tools

Porch, P~~atio~~
& Deck
Furnishings

COWLES
Creative Publishing, Inc.

Minnetonka, Minnesota, USA

Credits

Group Executive Editor: Paul Currie
Project Director: Mark Johanson
Associate Creative Director: Tim Himsel
Project Manager: Ron Bygness
Lead Project Designer: Jim Huntley
Editors: Mark Biscan, Steve Meyer
Editor & Technical Artist: Jon Simpson
Art Director: Gina Seeling
Contributing Art Directors: Ruth Eischens,
  John Hermansen, Geoffrey Kinsey
Technical Production Editor: Greg Pluth
Project Designers: Steve Meyer, Rob
  Johnstone, Greg Pluth
Project Manager Assistant: Andrew Sweet

*Vice President of Development Planning &
  Production:* Jim Bindas
Copy Editor: Janice Cauley
Shop Supervisor: Phil Juntti
Lead Builder: Rob Johnstone
Builders: Jon Hegge, Troy Johnson,
  John Nadeau
Production Staff: Helen Choralic, Tom Heck,
  Laura Hokkanen, Tom Hoops, Jeanette
  Moss, Andrew Mowery, Michelle Peterson,
  Mike Schauer, Kay Wethern

Director of Photography: Mike Parker
Creative Photo Coordinator:
  Cathleen Shannon
Studio Manager: Marcia Chambers
Lead Photographer: Alex Bachnick
Photographer: Rebecca Schmitt
Production Manager: Stasia Dorn
Printed on American paper by:
  Inland Press
  00 99 98 97 / 5 4 3 2 1

Creative Publishing, Inc.
  Minnetonka, Minnesota, USA

President: Iain Macfarlane
Executive V.P.: William B. Jones
Group Director, Book Development:
Zoe Graul

Created by: The editors of Cowles
Creative Publishing, in cooperation
with Black & Decker. ●BLACK&DECKER is a
trademark of the Black & Decker
Corporation and is used under license.

Library of Congress
Cataloging-in-Publication Data

Porch, patio & deck furnishings.
        p. cm.—(Portable Workshop)
  At head of title: Black & Decker
  ISBN   0-86573-690-1 (hardcover).

1. Outdoor furniture— Amateurs' manuals. 2. Furniture
making—Amateurs' manuals.
I. Cy DeCosse Incorporated
II. Series.
TT197.5.09P67 1996
684.1' 8—dc20   95-49810

Contents

Introduction

Everyone loves to spend time in the great outdoors—so much so that we build elaborate porches, patios and decks just so we have a convenient place to entertain friends, to relax or play with our families, or to enjoy a quiet, sunny afternoon with a good book and a cool drink. But without useful and attractive furnishings, even the nicest deck in the world is only a flat, empty space. The projects you can build using this book are designed to help you enjoy your porch, patio or deck to its full potential.

Porch, Patio & Deck Furnishings does what no other book of wood projects for outdoors can do. It gives you all the information you need to build the projects that you really want, but without assuming that you are an accomplished woodworker with a big shop full of fancy tools. Every project in this book can be built using only basic hand tools and portable power tools that you use regularly around your house: usually, only a circular saw, a jig saw, a sander and a drill.

You don't need a lot of experience working with basic hand and power tools to make these projects. But if you haven't used any of the tools before, it is a good idea to practice using them on scraps of wood before you tackle the actual project.

This is a book of plans. For each of the 20 projects that follow, you will find a complete cutting list, a lumber-shopping list, a detailed construction drawing, full-color photographs of major steps, and clear, easy-to-follow directions that guide you through every step of the project.

The Black & Decker® *Portable Workshop*™ series gives weekend do-it-yourselfers the power to build beautiful wood projects. Ask your local bookseller for information on other volumes in this innovative new series.

Organizing Your Worksite

Portable power tools and hand tools offer a level of convenience that is a great advantage over stationary power tools. But using them safely and conveniently requires some basic housekeeping. Whether you are working in a garage, a basement or outdoors, it is important that you establish a flat, dry holding area where you can store tools. Set aside a piece of plywood on sawhorses, or dedicate an area of your workbench for tool storage, and be sure to return tools to that area once you are finished with them. It is also important that all waste, including lumber scraps and sawdust, be disposed of in a timely fashion. Check with your local waste disposal department before throwing away any large scraps of building materials or any finishing-material containers.

Safety Tips
•Always wear eye and hearing protection when operating power tools and performing any other dangerous activities.
•Choose a well-ventilated work area when cutting or shaping wood and when using finishing products.

Tools & Materials

At the start of each project, you will find a set of symbols that show which power tools are used to complete the project as it is shown (see below). In some cases, optional power tools, like a compound miter saw, may be suggested for speedier work. You will also need a set of basic hand tools: a hammer, screwdrivers, tape measure, a level, a combination square, C-clamps, and pipe or bar clamps. Where required, specialty hand tools may be suggested within each article. You also will find a shopping list of all the construction materials you will need. Miscellaneous materials and hardware are listed at the bottom of the cutting list that accompanies the construction drawing. When buying lumber, keep in mind that the "nominal" size of the lumber is usually larger than the "actual size." For example, a 2 × 4 is actually 1½" × 3½".

Power Tools You Will Use

Circular saw *to make straight cuts. For long cuts and rip-cuts, use a straight-edge guide. Install a carbide-tipped combination blade for most projects.*

Drills: *use a cordless drill for drilling pilot holes and counterbores, and to drive screws; use an electric drill for sanding and grinding tasks.*

Jig saw *for making contoured cuts and internal cuts. Use a combination wood blade for most projects where you will cut pine, cedar or plywood.*

Power sander *to prepare wood for a finish and to smooth out sharp edges. Owning several power sanders (⅓-sheet, ¼-sheet, and belt) is helpful.*

Router *to cut decorative edges and roundovers in wood. As you gain more experience, use routers for cutting grooves (like dadoes) to form joints.*

Guide to Building Materials Used in this Book

•Sheet goods:
ABX PLYWOOD: *An exterior-grade plywood with a cabinet-grade face and a sanded face. Moderately expensive.*
BCX PLYWOOD: *An exterior-grade plywood with one sanded and filled face suitable for painting. Inexpensive.*
CEDAR PLYWOOD: *A naturally weather-resistant product, usually with one rough-sawn face. Moderately expensive.*
MDO PLYWOOD (SIGNBOARD): *Has moisture-resistant paper facing designed for painting. Moderately expensive.*
TILEBOARD: *Thin hardboard with a moisture-resistant surface (sometimes with decorative patterns). Inexpensive.*

•Dimension lumber:
SELECT PINE: *Finish-quality pine that is mostly free from knots and other imperfections (compared to #2 and #3 grades, which are rougher and have more knots). Relatively inexpensive.*
PRESSURE-TREATED PINE: *Pine, usually 2" or more in thickness, treated with wood preservative. Inexpensive.*
SELECT CEDAR: *Naturally moisture-resistant, mostly knot-free, smooth on both faces. Moderately expensive.*
#3 CEDAR: *Rough-sawn on one face for a rustic look, contains knots and other imperfections. Inexpensive.*

Guide to Fasteners & Adhesives Used in this Book

•Fasteners & Hardware:
GALVANIZED DECK SCREWS: *Sold in a wide range of lengths. Self-tapping. Excellent for use with a power driver.*
BRASS WOOD SCREWS: *Used for finer work, usually with a thicker shank than deck screws.*
NAILS & BRADS: *Choose galvanized or brass.*
HARDWARE: *Use galvanized, brass, or plastic hardware; look for "exterior-rated" notation on package.*

•Adhesives:
MOISTURE-RESISTANT GLUE: *Any exterior wood glue, such as plastic resin glue (plain yellow wood glue is not exterior-rated).*
HOT-MELT GLUE: *Applied with a hot-melt glue gun at joints that do not require high strength.*
TILEBOARD ADHESIVE: *Used to install tileboard (see above).*

Finishing Your Project

Before applying finishing materials like stain or paint, fill all nail holes and blemishes with wood putty or filler. Also, fill all voids in the edges of any exposed plywood with wood putty. Sand the dried putty smooth. Sand wood surfaces with medium-grit sandpaper (80 to 120), then finish-sand with fine sandpaper (150 to 180 grit). Wipe off residue with a rag dipped in mineral spirits before applying the finish. Most projects in this book are finished with clear wood sealer (right). For painted projects, use a good exterior primer, then apply exterior paint.

Patio Table

*This patio table blends sturdy construction with rugged style
to offer many years of steady service.*

CONSTRUCTION MATERIALS

Quantity	Lumber
2	4 × 4" × 10' cedar
2	2 × 2" × 10' cedar
2	1 × 4" × 8' cedar
3	1 × 6" × 8' cedar

Everyone knows a shaky, unstable patio table is a real headache, but you needn't be concerned about wobbly legs with this patio table. It is designed for sturdiness, with a close eye kept on style. As a result, this table will be a welcome addition to any backyard patio or deck.

This all-cedar patio table is roomy enough to seat six, and strong enough to support a large patio umbrella—even in high wind. The legs and cross-braces are cut from solid 4 × 4 cedar posts, then lag-bolted together. If you can find it at your local building center, buy heartwood cedar posts. Heartwood, cut from the center of the tree, is valued for its density, straightness, and resistance to decay. Because it is an eating surface, we applied a natural, clear linseed-oil finish.

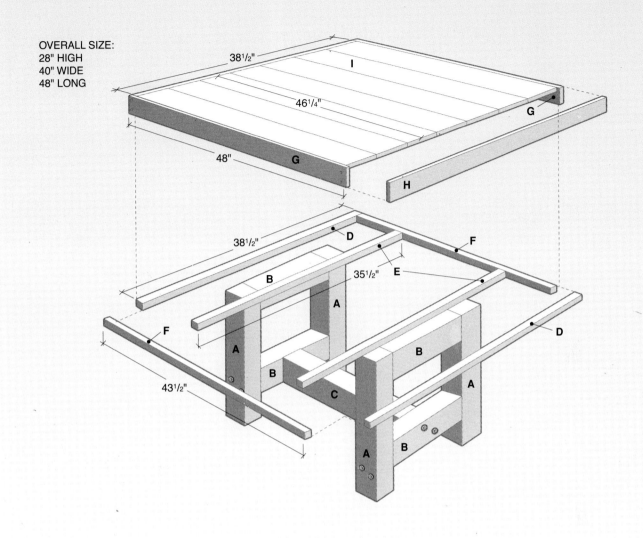

OVERALL SIZE:
28" HIGH
40" WIDE
48" LONG

Cutting List				
Key	Part	Dimension	Pcs.	Material
A	Leg	3½ × 3½ × 27¼"	4	Cedar
B	Stretcher	3½ × 3½ × 20"	4	Cedar
C	Spreader	3½ × 3½ × 28"	1	Cedar
D	End cleat	1½ × 1½ × 38½"	2	Cedar
E	Cross cleat	1½ × 1½ × 35½"	2	Cedar

Cutting List				
Key	Part	Dimension	Pcs.	Material
F	Side cleat	1½ × 1½ × 43½"	2	Cedar
G	Side rail	¾ × 3½ × 48"	2	Cedar
H	End rail	¾ × 3½ × 38½"	2	Cedar
I	Top slat	¾ × 5½ × 46½"	7	Cedar

Materials: Moisture-resistant glue, deck screws (2", 2½"), (12) ⅜ × 6" lag bolts with washers, finishing materials.

Note: Measurements reflect the actual size of dimensional lumber.

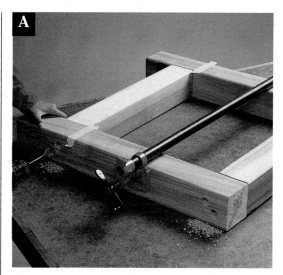

Counterbore two sets of holes on each leg to recess the lag bolts when you attach the legs to the stretchers.

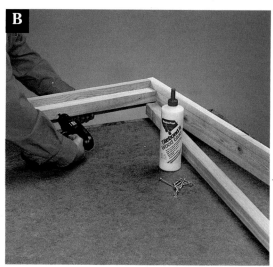

Maintain a ¾" distance from the top edge of the rails to the top edge of the cleats.

Directions: Patio Table

PREPARE THE LEG ASSEMBLY. Start by cutting the legs (A), stretchers (B) and spreader (C) to size from 4 × 4 cedar. Measure and mark 4" up from the bottom edge of each leg. These points mark the positions of the bottom edges of the lower stretchers. Test-fit the legs and stretchers to make sure they are square. The top stretchers should be flush against the top leg edges. Carefully position the pieces and clamp them together with pipe clamps. The metal jaws on the pipe clamps can damage the wood, so use protective clamping pads.

BUILD THE LEG ASSEMBLY. To complete this step, simply

attach the legs to the stretchers, then connect the spreader to the stretchers. Start by drilling ⅞ × ⅜"-deep counterbored holes centered diagonally across the top end of each leg and opposite the lower stretchers **(photo A)**. Drill ¼"-dia. pilot holes through each counterbored hole into the stretchers. Unclamp the pieces and drill ⅜"-dia. holes for lag bolts through the legs, using the pilot holes for center marks. Apply moisture-resistant glue to the

Use pencils or dowels to set even gaps between top slats. Tape slats in position with masking tape.

ends of the stretchers, and attach the legs to the stretchers by driving ⅜ × 6" galvanized lag bolts with washers through the legs into the stretchers. Attach the spreader to the stretchers in the same way.

ATTACH THE CLEATS AND RAILS. Cut the side rails (G) and end rails (H) to size from 1 × 4 cedar. Drill two evenly spaced pilot holes for countersunk 2" deck screws through the ends of the side rails. Apply glue and

---

TIP

Buy or make wood plugs to fill screw holes and conceal screw heads. Building centers and woodworker's stores usually carry a variety of plug types in several sizes and styles. To cut your own wood plug, you can either use a special-purpose plug-cutting tool (sold at woodworker's stores), or a small hole saw that mounts to your power drill (sold at building centers). The diameter of the plug must match the counterbore drilled into the wood.

Fasten cross cleats to the tabletop for strength, and to provide an anchor for the leg assembly.

Keep a firm grip on the tabletop slats when drilling deck screws through the cleats.

Before you stain or treat the patio table, sand the surfaces smooth.

fasten the side rails to the end rails with the screws. Cut the end cleats (D), cross cleats (E) and side cleats (F) from 2 × 2 cedar. Fasten the end cleats to the end rails ¾" below the top edges of the rails with glue and 2" deck screws **(photo B).** Repeat this procedure with the side cleats and side rails.

CUT & ATTACH THE TOP SLATS. Cut the top slats (I) to size from 1 × 6 cedar. Lay the slats into the tabletop frame so they rest on the cleats. Carefully spread

the slats apart so they are evenly spaced. Use masking tape to hold the slats in place once you achieve the correct spacing **(photo C).** Stand the tabletop frame on one end, and fasten the top slats in place by driving 2" deck screws up through the end cleats into the slats, one at a time **(photo D).** Make sure you hold or clamp each slat firmly while fastening, or the screws will push the slats away from the frame.

CONNECT THE LEGS AND TOP. To complete the assembly of this project, turn the tabletop over and center the legs on the underside. Make sure that the legs are the same distance apart at the tabletop as they are at the bottom. Lay the cross cleats across the inside of the table legs. Use 2½" deck screws to fasten the cross cleats to the tabletop **(photo E),** then use 3" deck screws to fasten the cross cleats to the legs.

FINISH THE PATIO TABLE. For a more finished appearance, fill the exposed screw holes with cedar plugs or buttons (see *Tip,* previous page), and smooth the edges of the table and legs with a sander or router. If you want to fit the table with a patio umbrella, simply use a 1½"-dia. hole saw to cut a hole into the center of the tabletop. Use a drill and spade bit to cut the 1½"-diameter hole through the spreader. Sand the patio table to finished smoothness **(photo F).** Finish the table as desired— we used clear linseed oil for a natural, protective finish that is non-toxic.

Garden Bench

Graceful lines and trestle construction make this bench a charming complement to porches, patios and decks—as well as gardens.

Quantity	Lumber
1	2 × 8" × 6' cedar
4	2 × 2" × 10' cedar
1	2 × 4" × 6' cedar
1	2 × 6" × 10' cedar
1	2 × 2" × 6' cedar
1	1 × 4" × 12' cedar

CONSTRUCTION MATERIALS

Casual seating is a welcome addition to any outdoor setting. This lovely garden bench tucks neatly around the borders of any porch, patio or deck to create a pleasant resting spot for as many as three adults, without taking up a lot of space. Or, station this garden bench near your rear entry to use as convenient seating for removing shoes or setting down grocery bags while you unlock the door.

The straightforward design of this bench lends itself to accessorizing. Station a rustic cedar planter next to the bench for a lovely effect. Or add a framed lattice trellis to one side to cut down on wind and direct sun.

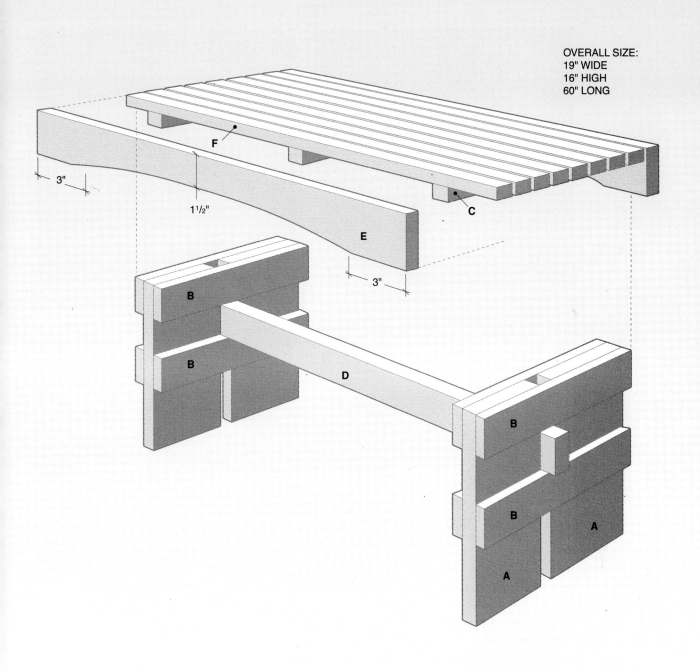

OVERALL SIZE:
19" WIDE
16" HIGH
60" LONG

3"

1½"

3"

F

C

E

B

B

D

B

B

A

A

Cutting List				
Key	**Part**	**Dimension**	**Pcs.**	**Material**
A	Leg half	1½ × 7¼ × 14½"	4	Cedar
B	Cleat	¾ × 3½ × 16"	8	Cedar
C	Brace	1½ × 1½ × 16"	3	Cedar
D	Trestle	1½ × 3½ × 60"	1	Cedar
E	Apron	1½ × 5½ × 60"	2	Cedar
F	Slat	1½ × 1½ × 60"	8	Cedar

Materials: Wood glue, wood sealer or stain, 3" wood screws, deck screws (1¼", 2").

Note: Measurements reflect the actual size of dimensional lumber.

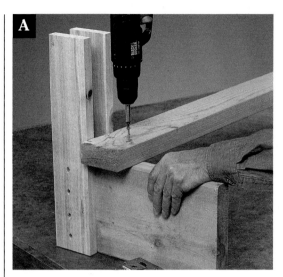

Make sure the stretcher is positioned correctly against the cleats, and attach it to the leg.

Attach the remaining leg half to the cleats on both ends to complete the leg assembly.

Directions: Arbor Bench

BUILD THE BASE. The base for this bench is composed of two sets of leg pairs connected by a full-length 2 × 4 trestle. Cut the leg halves (A), cleats (B) and trestle (D) to size. Start the assembly process by sandwiching one leg half between two cleats so the cleats are flush with the top and the outside edge of the leg half. Join the parts by driving four 1½" deck screws through each cleat and into the leg half, then assemble two more cleats with a leg half in the same fashion. Stand the two assemblies on end, with the open ends of the cleats pointing upward. Arrange the assemblies so they are roughly 4' apart, then set the trestle onto the inner edges of the leg halves, pressed flush against the bottoms of the cleats. Adjust the position of the assemblies so the trestle overhangs the leg half by 1½" at each end.

Attach the outer brace for the seat slats directly to the inside faces of the cleats.

Fasten the trestle to each leg half with glue and 2½" deck screws **(photo A).** Attach another pair of cleats to each leg half directly below the first pair, positioned so each cleat is snug against the bottom of the trestle. Now, slide the other leg half between the cleats, keeping the top edge flush with the upper cleats. Join the leg halves with the cleats using glue and 2½" deck screws **(photo B).** Cut the braces (C) from 2 × 2 cedar, then fasten

one brace to the inner top cleat on each leg assembly, so all tops are flush **(photo C).**

MAKE THE APRONS. The graceful arch cut into each apron gives the bench some character. Begin to make the seat frame by cutting the aprons to size from 2 × 6 cedar. Lay out the arch onto one apron, starting 3" from each end. The peak of the arch, located over the midpoint of the apron, should be 1½" up from the bottom edge. To draw a smooth, even arch onto the apron, drive a casing nail at the peak of the arch, then drive nails at the starting points of the arch. Slip a flexible ruler behind the nails at the starting points and in front of the nail at the peak to create a smooth arch. Trace along the inside of the ruler to make a cutting line **(photo D).** Cut along the cutting line with a jig saw, then smooth out the cut with a sander. Trace the profile of the arch onto the other apron, then make and sand the cut. Once both aprons are sanded smooth, cut the slats to length from cedar 2 × 2s. Attach one slat to the top, inside edge of each apron with glue and deck screws **(photo E).**

INSTALL THE SEAT SLATS. Fasten the third brace (C) between the aprons, centered end to end on the project. Make sure the top of the brace is flush with the tops of the aprons. Position the six remaining slats on the braces so the gaps between slats are even (½"-thick spacers help maintain the even gaps). Attach the slat

with glue and 2½" deck screws driven up through the braces and into each slat **(photo F).**

APPLY THE FINISHING TOUCHES. Sand the seat slats with progressively finer sandpaper (start with 100-grit, sand up to 150-grit) to create a nice, smooth surface that is free of splinters. Wipe away the sanding residue with a rag dipped in mineral spirits. Let the bench dry completely, then apply whichever finish you choose. We used clear wood sealer to protect the cedar in our bench without altering the color. You

TIP

Sometimes our best efforts produce furniture that wobbles because it is not quite level. One old trick for leveling furniture is to set a plastic wading pool on a flat plywood surface that is set to an exact level position with shims. Fill the pool with about ¼" of water. Set the furniture in the pool, then remove it quickly. Mark the tops of the waterlines on the legs, and use them as cutting lines for trimming the legs to level.

may prefer to use a wood stain first, but a protective coating is a good idea for any wood project that will be exposed to the elements.

Use a flexible ruler pinned between casing nails to trace a smooth arch onto the aprons.

Attach a 2 × 2 slat to the top, inside edge of each apron, using 2½" deck screws and glue.

Attach the seat slats with glue and 2½" deck screws. Insert ½"-thick spacers to set gaps between the slats.

Trellis Seat

Spice up your patio or deck with this sheltered seating structure. Set it in a secluded corner to create a warm, inviting outdoor living space.

CONSTRUCTION MATERIALS

Quantity	Lumber
1	4 × 4" × 6' cedar
2	2 × 8" × 8' cedar
4	2 × 4" × 12' cedar
1	1 × 6" × 10' cedar
8	1 × 2" × 8' cedar
2	½" × 4 × 4' cedar lattice

Made of lattice and cedar boards, our trellis seat is ideal for quiet moments of reading or conversing. The lattice creates just the right amount of privacy for a small garden or patio. It's an unobtrusive structure that is sure to add some warmth to your patio or deck. Position some outdoor plants along the top cap or around the frame sides to dress up the project and bring nature a little closer to home. For a cleaner appearance, conceal visible screw heads on the seat by counterboring the pilot holes for the screws and inserting cedar plugs (available at most woodworking stores) into the counterbores.

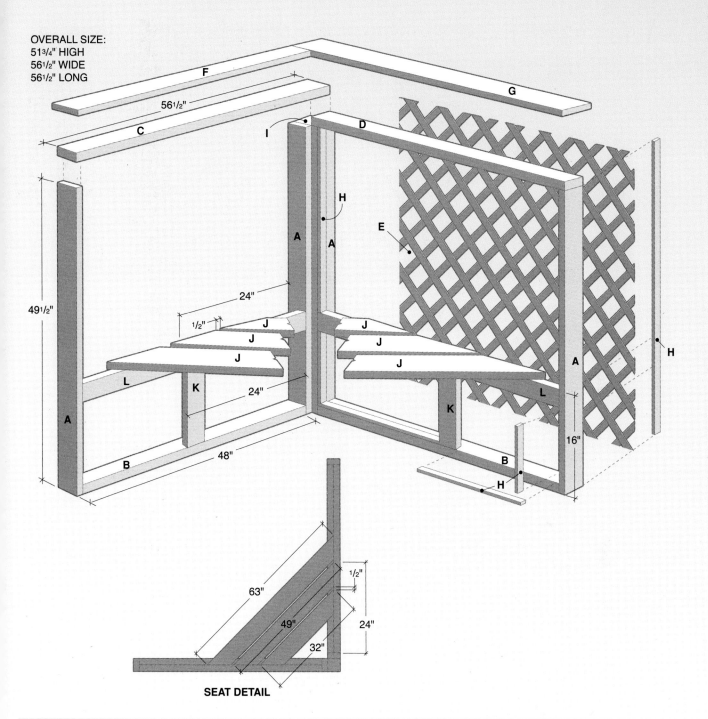

OVERALL SIZE:
51¾" HIGH
56½" WIDE
56½" LONG

F
56½"
C
I
D
49½"
24"
½"
A
A
A
H
E
J
J
J
J
J
J
J
J
L
K
24"
L
A
16"
A
B
48"
K
B
H
G

SEAT DETAIL

63"
49"
½"
24"
32"

Cutting List				
Key	**Part**	**Dimension**	**Pcs.**	**Material**
A	Frame side	1½ × 3½ × 49½"	4	Cedar
B	Frame bottom	1½ × 3½ × 48"	2	Cedar
C	Long rail	1½ × 3½ × 56½"	1	Cedar
D	Short rail	1½ × 3½ × 51"	1	Cedar
E	Lattice	½ × 4 × 4'	2	Cedar
F	Short cap	¾ × 5½ × 51"	1	Cedar

Cutting List				
Key	**Part**	**Dimension**	**Pcs.**	**Material**
G	Long cap	¾ × 5½ × 56½"	1	Cedar
H	Retaining strip	¾ × 1½" cut to fit	20	Cedar
I	Post	3½ × 3½ × 49½"	1	Cedar
J	Seat board	1½ × 7¼ × *	3	Cedar
K	Brace	1½ × 3½ × 11"	2	Cedar
L	Seat support	1½ × 3½ × 48"	2	Cedar

Materials: Moisture-resistant glue, deck screws (1¼", 2", 2½", 3"), finishing materials.

Note: Measurements reflect the actual size of dimensional lumber.

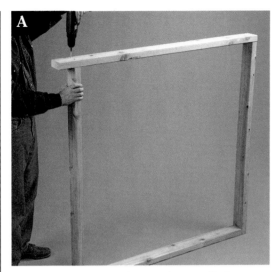

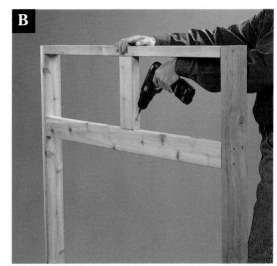

Attach the long rail at the top of one trellis frame with a 3½" overhang at one end to cover the post.

Drive deck screws toe-nail style through the braces and into the seat supports.

Directions: Trellis Seat

MAKE THE TRELLIS FRAMES. The trellis seat is constructed by joining two frames to a centrally-located post, then laying seat boards across the corner. Start by cutting the frame sides (A), frame bottoms (B), long rail (C), short rail (D), braces (K) and seat supports (L) from 2 × 4 cedar. Attach the frame sides to the frame bottoms with glue and two evenly-spaced 2½" deck screws, driven through counterbored ³⁄₁₆"-dia. pilot holes at the tops and bottoms of the frame sides. Attach the long and short rails to the tops of the frame sides with glue and deck screws driven through pilot holes in the top faces of the rails, and into the ends of the frame sides. The long rail should extend 3½" past one end of the frame **(photo A).** Measure and mark points 22¼" from each end on the frame bottoms to indicate position for the spacers. Position the braces flush with the inside frame bottom edges, and attach the pieces by driving 3" deck screws through pilot holes in the frame bottoms and into the ends of the braces. Position the seat supports 16" up from the bottoms of the frame bottoms, resting on the braces. Make sure the seat supports are flush with the inside edges of the braces, then attach with glue and counterbored 3" deck screws driven through the frame sides and into the ends of the seat supports. Finally, attach the braces to the seat supports by drilling angled ³⁄₁₆"-dia. pilot holes through each brace

Fasten the trellis frames to the post at right angles.

edge. Drive 3" deck screws toe-nail style through the braces and into the top edges of the seat supports **(photo B).**

JOIN THE TRELLIS FRAMES TO THE POST. Now, connect the two trellis frames to the 4 × 4 post. Cut the post (I) to length. Attach the two frame sections to the post by driving evenly spaced, counterbored 3" deck screws through the frame sides into the post **(photo C).** Make sure the overhang of the long rail fits snugly over the top of the post.

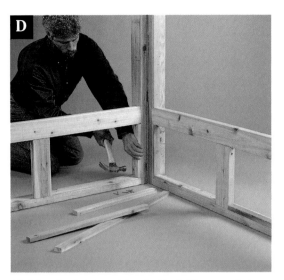

Nail 1 × 2 retaining strips for the lattice panels to the inside faces of the trellis frames.

Fasten the lattice panels to the seat supports with 1¼" deck screws, then attach outer retaining strips.

ATTACH THE LATTICE RETAINING STRIPS. The 1 × 2 lattice retaining strips (H) hold the lattice panels in place in the trellis frames. Cut retaining strips to fit along the inside faces of the trellis frames (but not the seat supports or braces). Nail the strips to the frames, flush with the inside frame edges, using 4d galvanized casing nails **(photo D).**

CUT & INSTALL THE LATTICE PANELS. Cutting the lattice panels is a simple procedure. Since you will probably be cutting through some metal fasteners in the lattice, fit your circular saw with a remodeler's blade. Sandwich the lattice panel between two boards near the cutting line to prevent the lattice from separating. Clamp the boards and the panel together, and cut the lattice panels to size. Always wear protective eyewear when operating power tools. Position the panels into the frames against the retaining strips, and attach them to the seat supports with 1¼" deck screws **(photo E).** Secure the panels by cutting re-

taining strips to fit along the outer edges of the inside faces of the trellis frame, then nailing the retaining strips in place.

BUILD THE SEAT. Cut the seat boards (J) from three pieces of 2 × 8 cedar. On a flat work surface, lay the seat boards together, edge-to-edge. Insert ½"-wide spacers between the boards, creating ½"-wide gaps. Draw cutting lines to lay out the seat shape onto the boards as if they were one board (see *Seat Detail,* page 17, for seat board dimensions). Gang-cut the seat boards to their finished size and shape with a circular saw. Attach the seat boards to the seat supports with evenly-spaced deck screws, maintaining the ½"-wide gap. Smooth the edges of the seat boards with a sander or router.

INSTALL TOP CAPS. The cap boards create handy shelves at the tops of the trellis frames. Cut the short cap (F) and long cap (G), then attach the caps to the tops of the long and short rails with deck screws **(photo F).**

APPLY FINISHING TOUCHES. We simply brushed on a coat of clear wood sealer to help preserve our project.

Attach the long and short caps to the tops of the trellis frames. The long cap overlaps the long rail and the post.

Outdoor Storage Center

*Create additional storage space for backyard games and equipment
with this efficient outdoor storage center.*

CONSTRUCTION MATERIALS

Quantity	Lumber
2	⅜" × 4 × 8' textured cedar plywood siding
2	¾" × 2 × 4' BC fir plywood handy panels
2	1 × 2" × 8' cedar
6	1 × 3" × 8' rough-sawn cedar
2	1 × 4" × 8' rough-sawn cedar
1	2 × 2" × 8' pine
1	1 × 2" × 8' pine

Sturdy cedar construction and a rustic appearance make this storage center an excellent addition to any backyard or outdoor setting. The top lid flips up for quick and easy access to the upper shelf storage area, while the bottom doors swing open to grant access to the lower storage compartments. The raised bottom shelf keeps all stored items up off the ground where they stay safe and dry. Lawn chairs, yard games, grilling supplies, fishing and boating equipment, and much more, can be easily kept out of sight and protected from the weather. If security is a concern, simply add a locking hasp and padlock to the top lid to keep your life jackets and horseshoe games safe from unwanted guests. If you have a lot of traffic in and out of the top compartment, add lid support hardware to prop the lid open.

OVERALL SIZE:
23¹/₂" WIDE
43³/₈" HIGH
48" LONG

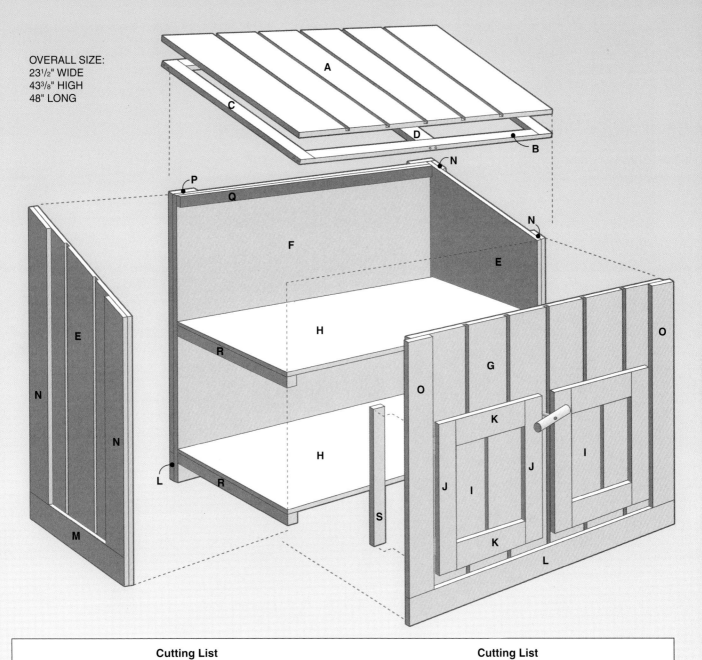

Cutting List				
Key	Part	Dimension	Pcs.	Material
A	Lid	⅝ × 24 × 48"	1	Plywood siding
B	Lid edge	¾ × 1½ × 45"	2	Cedar
C	Lid end	¾ × 1½ × 24"	2	Cedar
D	Lid stringer	¾ × 2½ × 21"	1	Cedar
E	End panel	⅝ × 22 × 42"	2	Plywood siding
F	Back panel	⅝ × 44¾ × 42"	1	Plywood siding
G	Front panel	⅝ × 44¾ × 37½"	1	Plywood siding
H	Shelf	¾ × 20¾ × 44¾"	2	Fir plywood
I	Door panel	⅝ × 15¾ × 17¾"	2	Plywood siding
J	Door stile	¾ × 3½ × 21¼"	4	Cedar

Cutting List				
Key	Part	Dimension	Pcs.	Material
K	Door rail	¾ × 3½ × 12¼"	4	Cedar
L	Kickboard	¾ × 2½ × 47½"	2	Cedar
M	End plate	¾ × 2½ × 22"	2	Cedar
N	End trim	¾ × 2½ × 39½"	4	Cedar
O	Front trim	¾ × 2½ × 35"	2	Cedar
P	Back trim	¾ × 2½ × 39½"	2	Cedar
Q	Hinge cleat	¾ × 1½ × 44¾"	1	Pine
R	Shelf cleat	1½ × 1½ × 20¾"	4	Pine
S	Door cleat	¾ × 1½ × 18"	2	Pine

Materials: Moisture-resistant glue, (6) hinges, deck screws (1¼", 2½"), (2) door catches or a 1"-dia. × 12" dowel and a ¼"-dia. × 4" carriage bolt, finishing materials.

Note: All measurements reflect actual size of dimensional lumber.

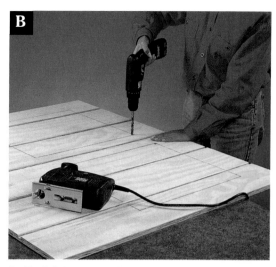

Cut and fasten the lid to the lid framework with the grooves in the panel running back to front.

Drill a ⅜"-dia. starter hole at a corner of each door opening and cut out the openings with a jig saw.

Directions:
Outdoor Storage Center

MAKE THE LID ASSEMBLY. Start by cutting the lid (A) from cedar sheet siding (we used siding with 8"-on-center channels) using a circular saw and a straightedge. Cut the lid edges (B) and lid ends (C) from 1 × 2 cedar, and cut the lid stringer (D) from 1 × 3 cedar. Lay the lid ends and edges on their faces, smooth side up, on a flat surface. Position the lid ends flush with the outsides of the lid edges. Fasten with glue and 2½" deck screws. Position the lid stringer midway between the lid ends, and glue and screw it in place. Apply glue to the top faces of the lid end, stringer, and lid edges. Set the lid on the frame assembly **(photo A)** and screw it in place with 1¼" deck screws.

MAKE THE PANELS. Start by cutting the back panel (F) and front panel (G) to size from cedar sheet siding. On the inside face of the front panel, measure up from the bottom and scribe straight lines at 5" and 23". Also measure in 4"

Attach the end panels to the back panel, keeping the back panel flush with the back edges of the end panels.

and 22" from each side and scribe lines. These square layout lines mark the cutout lines for the door openings. Next, drill a ⅜"-dia. starter hole at one corner in each door opening **(photo B).** Cut out the door openings with a jig saw and sand the edges smooth. Cut end panels (E) to size. On the front edge of each panel, measure down 4½" and place a mark. Draw a line connecting each mark with the top corner on the back edge of the panel, creating cross-cutting lines for

the back-to-front tapers on the side panels. Cross-cut along the lines with a circular saw.

CREATE THE PANEL ASSEMBLY. Stand the back panel on its bottom edge and butt it up between the end panels, flush with the back edges. Fasten the back panel between the side panels with glue and 1¼" screws **(photo C).**

BUILD & ATTACH THE SHELVES. Cut the shelves (H) to size from plywood. Measure up 25" from the bottoms of the end panels and draw reference marks for

Place the shelf on top of the cleats and fasten with glue and screws.

positioning the top shelf. Cut the shelf cleats (R) from 2 × 2 cedar. Attach the cleats just below the reference lines with glue and 1¼" screws driven through the end panels and into the cleats. Fasten the shelf to the cleats with 1¼" screws **(photo D).** Also drive screws through the back panel and into the back edge of the shelf. Mark reference lines for the bottom shelf, 4" up from the bottoms of the side panels. Install the bottom shelves the same way as the top shelves. Position the front panel (G) between the end panels and fasten with glue and screws.

CUT & INSTALL TRIM. Cut the kickboards (L) for the front and back, the end plates (M), the end trim (N), the front trim (O), and the back trim (P) from 1 × 3 rough-sawn cedar. Sand all ends smooth. Attach the end kick boards at the bases of the side panels, using counterbored deck screws. Next, attach the front and back kickboards to the bases of the front and back panels. Hold the end trim pieces in position against the side panels at both the front and back edges, and

trace the profile of the tapered side panels onto the trim pieces to make cutting lines (the trim pieces at the fronts should be flush with the front panel). Cut at the lines with a circular saw. Screw the end trim pieces to the side panels **(photo E).** Attach the front and back trim to the front and back panels, covering the edges of the end trim pieces.

ATTACH THE DOORS & LID. Cut the door stiles and door rails to size from 1 × 4 cedar, then attach them to the cutout door panels (I), forming a frame that extends 1¾" past the edges of the door panels on all sides. Cut 1 × 2 door cleats (S) to size and screw them to the inside faces of the front panel directly behind the hinge locations at the outside edges of the openings. Mount two butt hinges on the outside edge of each door, then screw the hinges to the front panel and hinge cleats. Install a door catch for each door (instead, we used a 1" dowel bolted to the front panel as a turnbuckle—see page 21). Mount the lid to the back panel and cleat with butt hinges.

APPLY FINISHING TOUCHES. Sand all edges smooth, then apply a coat of clear wood sealer, or any other finish of your choice.

Attach the end trim to the end panel, keeping the front edge of the trim flush with the face of the front panel.

Porch Swing

*You'll cherish the pleasant memories created
by this porch swing built for two.*

CONSTRUCTION MATERIALS

Quantity	Lumber
8	1 × 2" × 8' pine
1	1 × 4" × 4' pine
2	2 × 4" × 10' pine
1	2 × 6" × 10' pine

Nothing conjures up pleasant images of a cool summer evening like a porch swing. When the porch swing is one that you've built yourself, the images will be all the more pleasant. Our porch swing is made from sturdy pine to withstand years and years of memory making. The gentle curve of the slatted seat and the relaxed angle of the swing back are designed for your comfort. When you build your porch swing, pay close attention to the spacing of the rope holes drilled in the back, arms and seat of the swing. They are arranged to create perfect balance when you hang your swing from your porch ceiling.

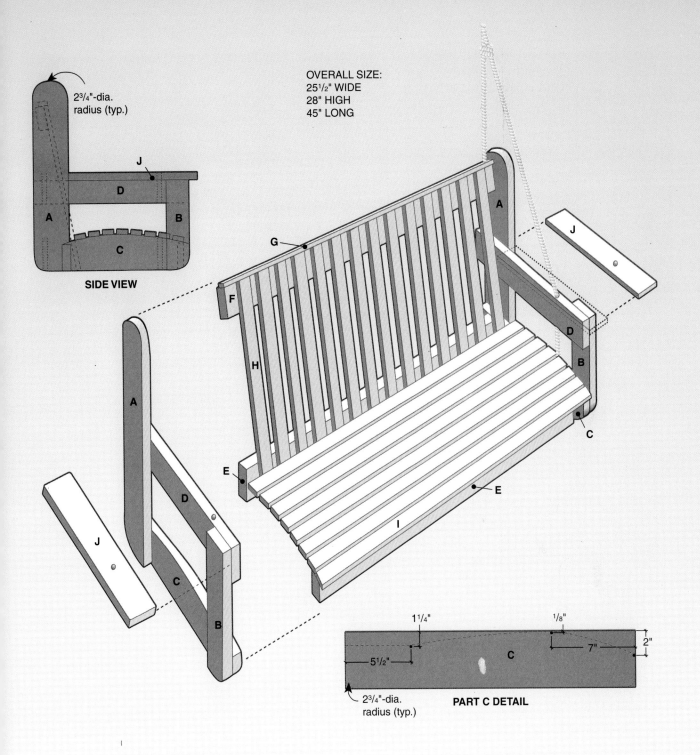

2³/₄"-dia. radius (typ.)

OVERALL SIZE:
25¹/₂" WIDE
28" HIGH
45" LONG

SIDE VIEW

1¹/₄"   ¹/₈"
5¹/₂"   7"   2"
C

2³/₄"-dia. radius (typ.)

PART C DETAIL

Cutting List

Key	Part	Dimension	Pcs.	Material
A	Back upright	1½ × 5½ × 28"	2	Pine
B	Front upright	1½ × 3½ × 13½"	2	Pine
C	Seat support	1½ × 5½ × 24"	2	Pine
D	Arm rail	1½ × 3½ × 24"	2	Pine
E	Stretcher	1½ × 3½ × 39"	2	Pine

Cutting List

Key	Part	Dimension	Pcs.	Material
F	Back cleat	1½ × 3½ × 42"	1	Pine
G	Top rail	¾ × 1½ × 42"	1	Pine
H	Back slat	¾ × 1½ × 25"	14	Pine
I	Seat slat	¾ × 1½ × 42"	8	Pine
J	Arm rest	¾ × 3½ × 20"	2	Pine

Materials: Wood glue, 20' of ½"-dia. nylon rope, wood screws (#8 x 2", #10 x 2½", #10 x 3").

Note: Measurements reflect the actual size of dimensional lumber.

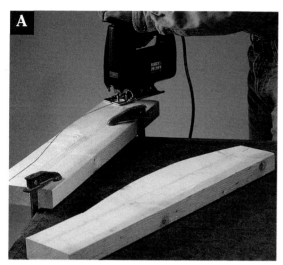

Use a jig saw to cut the contours into the tops of the seat supports.

Use a ⅝" spade bit and a right-angle drilling guide when drilling rope holes through the seat supports.

Directions: Porch swing

MAKE THE SEAT SUPPORTS. Cut the seat supports (C) from 2 × 6 stock. Use the pattern on page 25 as a pattern for laying out the contour on the top of one of the seat supports. Use a flexible ruler, bent to follow the contour, to ensure that the cutting line is smooth (see page 14). Cut along the cutting line with a jig saw **(photo A).** Sand the contour smooth with a drill and drum sander or with a belt sander, then use the contoured seat support as a template for marking a matching contour on the other seat support. Cut and sand the second seat support to match.

BUILD THE SEAT FRAME. Cut the arm rails (D), and stretchers (E) from 2 × 4 pine. Attach one of the stretchers between the seat supports, ¾" from the front edges and ½" from the bottom edges, using glue and #10 × 2½" wood screws. Fasten the other stretcher between the supports so the front face of the stretcher is 6" from the backs of the supports, and all bottom edges are flush. Use a ⅝" spade

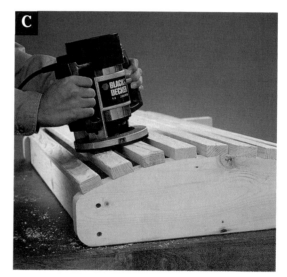

Smooth out the top exposed edges of the seat slats with a router and ¼" roundover bit (or use a power sander).

bit to drill guide holes for the ropes in the seat supports and the arm rails. Drill a hole 1½" from the back end of each piece, and also drill a hole 4½" from the front end of each piece. Use a right-angle drill guide to make sure holes stay centered all the way through **(photo B).**

INSTALL THE SEAT SLATS. Cut the seat slats (I) from 1 × 2 pine (make sure to buy full-sized 1 × 2s, not 1 × 2 furring strips). Arrange the slats across the seat supports, using ½"-thick spacers to make sure the gaps are even. The front slat should

overhang the front stretcher by about ¼", and the back slat should be flush with the front of the back stretcher. Fasten the slats to the seat support with glue and #8 × 2" wood screws (one screw at each slat end). Smooth the top edges of the slats with a router and ¼" roundover bit, or a power sander **(photo C).**

BUILD THE BACK. Cut the back cleat (F) from 2 × 4 pine, and cut the back slats (H) from 1 × 2 pine. Fasten the slats to the back cleat, leaving a 1½" gap at each end, and spacing the slats at regular 1½" intervals

Use 1 × 2 spacers to align the back slats, then fasten the slats to the back cleat.

Fasten the top rail to the back cleat, so the front edge of the rail is flush with the fronts of the slats.

Slide the back assembly against the seat assembly and attach.

(photo D). The tops of the slats should be flush with the top of the cleat. Cut the top rail (G) from 1 × 2 pine, and fasten it to the cleat so the front edge of the rail is flush with the fronts of the slats (photo E). Drill a ⅝"-dia. rope hole at each end of the top cleat, directly over the back holes in the arm rails.

ATTACH UPRIGHTS & ARM REST. Cut the back uprights (A) from 2 × 6 pine, and cut the front uprights (B) from 2 × 4 pine. Make a round profile cut at the tops of the back uprights (pattern, page 25), using a jig saw. Attach the uprights to the outside faces of the seat supports, flush with the ends of the supports. Use glue and two #10 × 3" wood screws at each joint. Slide the back slat assem-

bly behind the seat assembly (photo F), and screw the back cleat to the back uprights, so the upper rear corners of the cleat are flush with the back edges of the uprights. Attach the arm rails between the uprights, flush with the tops. Make sure the rope holes are aligned. Cut the arm rest (J) from 1 × 4 pine, then smooth the edges. Set the arm rests on the arm rail, centered side to side and flush against the back uprights. Mark the locations of the rope holes in the arm rails onto the arm rests, then drill matching holes into the arm rests. Attach arm rests to rails with glue and #8 × 2" screws.

APPLY FINISHING TOUCHES. Sand and paint the swing, then thread pieces of ½"-dia. nylon rope through all four sets of rope holes (see photo, page 24) and tie them to hang the swing.

TIP

Use heavy screw eyes driven into ceiling joists to hang porch swings. If the ropes don't line up with the ceiling joists, lag-screw a 2 × 4 cleat to the ceiling joists and attach screw eyes to the cleat.

Freestanding Arbor

Create a shady retreat on a sunny patio or deck with this striking arbor. The design features an Oriental flavor that will bring a taste of the exotic to any setting. So park your favorite bench or chair under the sheltering cedar of this arbor and let the relaxation begin.

This freestanding arbor combines the beauty and durability of natural cedar with an Oriental-inspired design. Set it up on your patio or deck, or in a quiet corner of your backyard, to add just the right finishing touch to turn your outdoor living space into a showplace geared for relaxation and quiet contemplation. The arbor has a long history as a focal point in gardens and other outdoor areas throughout the world. And if privacy and shade are concerns, you can enhance the sheltering quality by adding climbing vines that weave their way in and out of the trellis. Or simply set a few potted plants around the base to help the arbor blend in with the outdoor environment. Another way to integrate plantlife into your arbor is to hang decorative potted plants from the top beams.

This arbor is freestanding, so it can be moved to a new site easily whenever you desire. Or, you can anchor it permanently to a deck or to the ground and equip it with a built-in seat. Sturdy posts made from 2 × 4 cedar serve as the base of our arbor, forming a framework for a 2 × 2 trellis system that scales the sides and top. The curved cutouts that give the arbor its Oriental appeal are made with a jig saw, then smoothed out with a drill and drum sander for a more finished appearance.

CONSTRUCTION MATERIALS

Quantity	Lumber
2	1 × 2" × 8' cedar
5	2 × 2" × 8' cedar
9	2 × 4" × 8' cedar
3	2 × 6" × 8' cedar

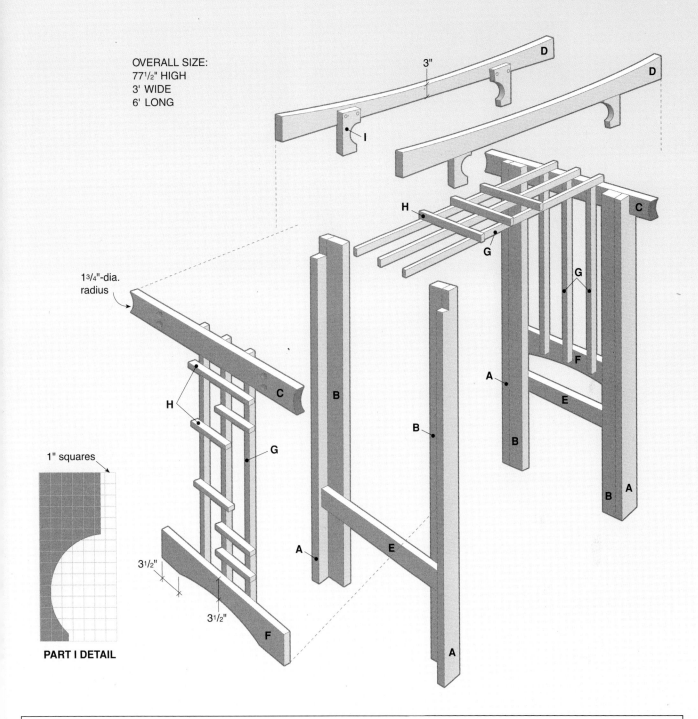

OVERALL SIZE:
77¹/₂" HIGH
3' WIDE
6' LONG

3"

D

D

I

1³/₄"-dia.
radius

H

C

B

B

A

E

A

G

H

G

C

G

A

B

B

A

F

E

B

1" squares

3¹/₂"

3¹/₂"

F

PART I DETAIL

Cutting List				
Key	**Part**	**Dimension**	**Pcs.**	**Material**
A	Leg front	1½ × 3½ × 6'	4	Cedar
B	Leg side	1½ × 3½ × 6'	4	Cedar
C	Cross beam	1½ × 3½ × 3'	2	Cedar
D	Top beam	1½ × 5½ × 6'	2	Cedar
E	Side rail	1½ × 3½ × 21"	2	Cedar

Cutting List				
Key	**Part**	**Dimension**	**Pcs.**	**Material**
F	Side spreader	1½ × 5½ × 21"	2	Cedar
G	Trellis strip	1½ × 1½ × 4'	9	Cedar
H	Cross strip	¾ × 1½ × *	15	Cedar
I	Brace	1½ × 5½ × 15"	4	Cedar

Materials: Wood glue, wood sealer or stain, #10 × 3" wood screws, deck screws (1¼", 2½"), finishing materials.

Note: Measurements reflect the actual size of dimensional lumber.

*Cut to fit

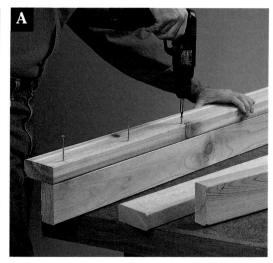

Create four legs by fastening leg sides to leg fronts at right angles.

Cut a notch in the top of each of the four legs to hold the cross beams.

Directions: Freestanding Arbor

MAKE THE LEGS. Each of the four arbor legs is made from two 6'-long pieces of 2 × 4 cedar, fastened at right angles with 3" deck screws. Cut the leg fronts (A) and leg sides (B), and position the leg sides and fronts so the top and bottom edges are flush. Apply moisture-resistant glue to the joint, and attach the leg fronts to the leg sides with evenly spaced screws driven through the faces of the fronts and into the edges of the sides **(photo A).** Then, use a jig saw to cut a 3½"-long × 2"-wide notch at the top outside corner of each leg front **(photo B).** These notches are made to cradle the cross beams when the arbor is assembled.

MAKE THE CROSS BEAMS, RAILS & SPREADERS. Begin this step by cutting both cross beams (C) to

A piece of cardboard acts as a template when you trace the outline for the arc on the cross beams.

length from 2 × 4s. For a decorative touch, cut a small arc at both ends of each cross beam. Simply use a compass to draw a 3½"-diameter semicircle at the edge of a strip of cardboard, cut out the semicircle, and use the strip as a template for marking the arcs **(photo C).** Cut out the arcs with a jig saw, then sand the cuts smooth with a drill and drum sander. The rails (E) are also cut from 2 × 4s. They are fitted between pairs of legs on each side of the arbor, near the bottom, to keep the ar-

bor square. Cut them to length. Also cut two spreaders (F) from 2 × 6 cedar—the spreaders fit just above the rails on each side. After cutting the spreaders to length, mark a curved cutting line on the bottom of each spreader (see diagram, page 29). To mark the cutting lines, draw starting points 3½" in from each end of a spreader, then make a reference line 2" up from the bottom of the spreader board. Tack a casing nail on the refer-

D

Lag-screw the cross beams to the legs, and fasten the spreaders and rails with deck screws to assemble the side frames.

E

Attach trellis strips to the cross brace and spreader with deck screws.

ence line, centered between the ends of the spreader. With the spreader clamped to the worksurface, also tack nails into the worksurface next to the starting lines on the spreader. Slip a thin strip of metal or plastic between the casing nails so the strip bows out to create a smooth arc. Trace the arc onto the spreader, then cut along the line with a jig saw. Smooth out with a drum sander, then use

the first spreader as a template for marking and cutting the second spreader (see page 14).

ASSEMBLE THE SIDE FRAMES. Each side frame consists of a front and back leg, joined together by a rail, spreader and a cross beam. Begin by laying two leg assemblies parallel on a worksurface, with the notched board in each leg facing up. Space the legs so the inside faces of the notched

boards are 21" apart. Set a cross beam into the notches, overhanging each leg by 6", and also set a spreader and a rail between the legs for spacing. Attach the cross beam to each leg with glue and two ⅜"-dia. × 2½" lag screws driven through counterbored pilot holes **(photo D).** Making sure to keep the legs parallel, use glue and countersunk 3" deck screws to fasten the rail and spreader between the legs. The top of the spreader should be 29½" up from the bottoms of the legs, and the top of the rail should be 18" up from the leg bottoms.

ATTACH THE SIDE TRELLIS PIECES. Our freestanding arbor contains a trellis on each side and at the top. Each side trellis is made from vertical strips of cedar 2 × 2 that are fastened to the side frames. Horizontal cross strips will be added later to create a decorative cross-hatching effect (page 33). Cut three vertical trellis strips (G) for each side frame, and attach them to the side frames so they are spaced 2⅜" apart, with the ends flush with the top of the cross beam **(photo E).** Use 2½" counterbored deck screws to attach the trellis strips to the cross beam and the spreader. Attach trellis strips to both side frames.

CUT & SHAPE THE TOP BEAMS. The top beams (D) link the two side frames, and feature a

TIP

Drill counterbores for lag screws in two stages: first, drill a pilot hole for the shank of the screw; then, use the pilot hole as a center to drill a counterbore for the washer and screw head.

Use long pieces of 1 × 4 to brace the side frames in an upright, level position while you attach the top beams.

Lock the legs in a square position after assembling the arbor by tacking strips of wood between the front legs and between the back legs.

sweeping arc design. Cut two top beams to length from 2 × 6 cedar. Draw 1½"-deep arcs at the bottom edges of the top beams, starting at the ends of each board (see *Assemble the Side Frames,* page 31). Cut the arcs into the top beams with a jig saw, and sand smooth with a drum sander.

TIP

There are no firm rules about arbor placement. It can be positioned to provide a focal point for a porch, patio or deck. Placed against a wall or at the end of a plain surface, arbors improve the general look of the area. With some thick, climbing vines and vegetation added to the arbor, you can also disguise a utility area such as a trash collection space.

ASSEMBLE THE TOP & THE SIDES. Because the side frames are fairly heavy and bulky, you will need to brace them in an upright position in order to fasten the top beams between them. A simple way to accomplish this is to use a pair of 1 × 4 braces to connect the tops and bottoms of the side frames **(photo F).** Clamp the ends of the braces to the side frames so the side frames are 4' apart, and use a level to make sure the side frames are plumb. Then, mark a centerpoint for a lag bolt 12¾" from each end of each top beam, and drill a ¼"-diameter pilot hole through that centerpoint. Set the top beams on top of the cross braces of the side frames, and use a pencil to mark the pilot hole locations onto the cross

beams. Remove the top beams and drill pilot holes through the cross beams. Counterbore the pilot holes, then secure the top beams to the cross beams with 6" lag bolts and washers. Cut four braces (I) to size, and transfer the brace cutout pattern from the diagram on page 29 to each board. Cut the patterns with a jig saw, then attach the braces at the joints where the leg fronts meet the top beams, using 2½" deck screws. To make sure the arbor assembly stays in position while you complete the project, attach 1 × 2 scraps between the front legs and between the back legs **(photo G).** Cut and attach three trellis strips (G) between the top beams (see *Attach the Side Trellis Pieces,* page 31).

Attach the trellis cross strips to spice up the design and assist climbing plants.

ADD TRELLIS CROSS STRIPS. The 1 × 2 cross strips that fit between the trellis strips on the sides and top are an important part of our distinctive arbor design. We cut the cross strips to 7" and 10" lengths, and installed them at 3" intervals in a staggered pattern **(photo H).** Feel free to adjust the sizes and placement of the cross strips if you prefer. But for best appearance, try to retain some symmetry of placement between the cross strips, and make sure that the strips that fit across the top trellis strips are arranged similarly to the side strips.

APPLY THE FINISHING TOUCHES. To protect the arbor, coat the cedar wood with clear wood sealer. After the finish dries, the arbor is ready to be placed onto your deck or patio, or in a quiet corner of your yard. Because of its sturdy construction, the arbor can simply be set onto a hard, flat surface and it is ready to begin duty. If you plan to install a permanent seat in the arbor, you should anchor it to the ground. The best way to anchor it depends on the type of surface it is resting on. For decks, try to position the arbor so you can

screw the legs to the rim of the deck, or toenail the legs into the deck boards. You can buy fabricated metal post stakes, available at most building centers, to anchor the arbor to the ground.

TIP

Create an arbor seat by resting two 2 × 10 cedar boards on the rails in each side frame. Overhang the rails by 6" or so, and drive a few 3" deck screws through the boards and into the rails to secure the seat.

Play Center

With this portable play center, children can have fun storing and organizing their toys right where they play with them.

CONSTRUCTION MATERIALS

Quantity	Lumber
1	¾" × 4 × 8' plywood
1	2 × 4" × 6' pine

Provide toddlers and young children with a clean, safe, easily accessible storage and play area with this efficient, portable play center. Built at heights that are comfortable for kids, the top shelves are meant to be used as play surfaces—they can even be fitted with plastic containers to hold sand, water, blocks or dolls. This unit is completely portable, so you can roll it onto the deck, plant it under a favorite shade tree, or park it on the backyard patio. And if the weather is not cooperating, you can bring it indoors to the family room. The play center is so simple to make, you may want to have the kids chip in and help you build it.

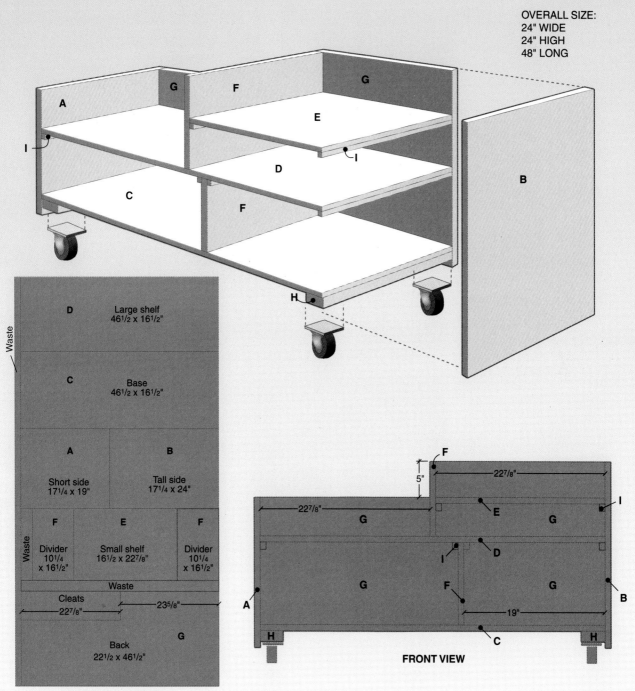

OVERALL SIZE:
24" WIDE
24" HIGH
48" LONG

CUTTING DIAGRAM

D — Large shelf 46½ x 16½"
C — Base 46½ x 16½"
A — Short side 17¼ x 19"
B — Tall side 17¼ x 24"
F — Divider 10¼ x 16½"
E — Small shelf 16½ x 22⅞"
F — Divider 10¼ x 16½"
Waste
Cleats — 22⅞" — 23⅝"
Waste
G — Back 22½ x 46½"

FRONT VIEW

5"
22⅞"
22⅞"
19"

Cutting List

Key	Part	Dimension	Pcs.	Material
A	Short side	¾ × 17¼ × 19"	1	MDO plywood
B	Tall side	¾ × 17¼ × 24"	1	MDO plywood
C	Base	¾ × 16½ × 46½"	1	MDO plywood
D	Large shelf	¾ × 16½ × 46½"	1	MDO plywood
E	Small shelf	¾ × 16½ × 22⅞"	1	MDO plywood

Cutting List

Key	Part	Dimension	Pcs.	Material
F	Divider	¾ × 16½ × 10¼"	2	MDO plywood
G	Back	¾ × 22½ × 46½"	1	MDO plywood
H	Base cleat	1½ × 3½ × 16"	2	Pine
I	Shelf cleat	¾ × ¾ × 16½"	6	MDO plywood

Materials: Moisture resistant glue, 1½" deck screws, tape measure, finishing materials, (4) locking casters.

Note: Measurements reflect the actual size of dimensional lumber.

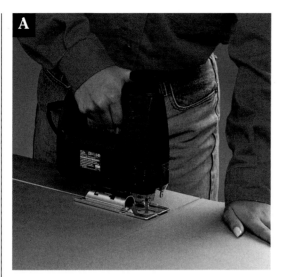

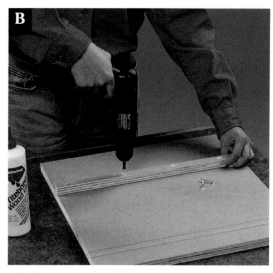

Use a jig saw to cut out a rectangular section of the back panel.

Attach cleats to the side panels at shelf locations.

Slip a divider between the base and the large shelf to support and compartmentalize the large shelf.

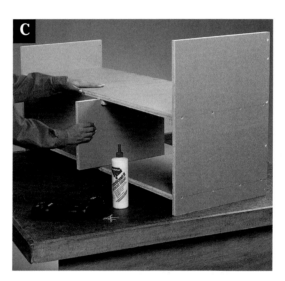

Directions:
Play Center

CUT THE SIDES, BACK & BASE. Except for the 2 × 4 caster supports, the parts for the play center all are cut from one sheet of ¾"-thick MDO plywood, also known as "signboard." MDO plywood is coated on both faces with a special paper that produces a superior painted finish that stands up to exposure to the elements of nature. Use a circular saw and a straightedge guide to cut plywood panels. Start by cutting the short side (A), tall side (B), base (C) and back (G) from MDO plywood. The base and sides are square pieces that require no further cutting. The back needs to be cut into an L-shape. After cutting the back panel to full size (see *Cutting List,* page 35), make layout lines for a rectangular cutout at one corner. Measure out 5" from the corner on the short side of the panel, and measure out 22⅞" on the long side of the panel. Extend the marks out onto the face of the panel, using a square, then cut out along the lines to the point of intersection, using a jig saw **(photo A).** Remove the rectangular cutout and sand the edges of the cutout area.

ATTACH CLEATS TO PANELS. Cut a long strip of plywood from a waste area (see *Cutting Diagram,* page 35), then cut the strip into six 16½"-long pieces to use as shelf cleats. Mark reference lines at the shelf height on the short side and tall side panels: on the inside faces of each side panel, draw a straight line 13" up from the bottom edge to mark shelf-cleat height for the large shelf; draw another straight line 5¾" down from the top of the tall side panel to mark the shelf-cleat height for the small shelf. Attach a cleat (I) just below each of these marks, using glue and 1¼" counterbored deck screws **(photo B).** Cut the base cleats (H) from a 2 × 4. Mark reference lines for the cleats 2" up from the bottom edge of each side panel. Attach the base cleats just below the reference lines with glue and counterbored 3" deck screws driven through the outside faces of the side panels and into the edges of the cleats.

TIP

Do not use coarse sandpaper on the faces of MDO plywood. Anything coarser than 100-grit can damage the paper facing.

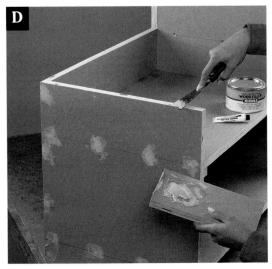

Fill screw holes and surface defects with exterior-rated wood filler or putty, then sand putty smooth.

Finish-sand the project with 220-grit sandpaper.

INSTALL THE BASE & LARGE SHELF. With the side panels propped in an upright position, set the base onto the base cleats so it is flush with the insides and front edges of the panels. Attach the base with glue and 1¼" counterbored deck screws driven through the outside faces of the side panels and into the edges of the base. Use four evenly spaced screws per side. Cut the large shelf (D), then set it on the shelf cleats on each side panel, making sure the front of the shelf is flush with the fronts of the side panels. Attach with glue and counterbored screws driven through the side panels and into the edges of the shelf.

ATTACH THE DIVIDERS. The dividers provide shelf support and create separate compartments within the play center for different kinds of toys or equipment. Cut the dividers (F). On one divider, mark a straight line 5¾" down from the top and install a shelf cleat for the small shelf just below the line. Glue two shelf cleats ¾" apart on the underside of the large shelf, cen-

tered around a mark 19" from the inside of the tall side panel. Once the glue dries, insert the cleatless divider between the cleats on the shelf **(photo C),** and attach with 1¼" deck screws driven through the shelf and base and into the edges of the divider. Attach the cleated divider to the top surface of the large shelf so the divider side with the cleat is 22⅞" away from the tall side panel. Cut the small shelf (E), set it on the cleats on the top divider and the tall side panel, and attach it with deck screws. Now position the back panel so it fits between the side panels, flush against the back edges of the shelves and dividers. Drive counterbored deck screws through the back panel and into the dividers and shelves. Also drive counterbored 1¼" deck screws through the side panels and into the edges of the back panel.

COMPLETE THE PLAY CENTER. Fill screw holes and plywood voids with wood putty **(photo D).** Sand the putty until it is level with the surrounding surface **(photo E),** then finish-sand the entire project with 220-grit sandpaper. Wipe off the sanding residue with a rag dipped in mineral spirits, then apply a coat of exterior primer to all surfaces. After the primer dries, paint the play center with exterior paint that dries to an enamel finish **(photo F).** Attach a locking caster near both ends of each base cleat.

Prime and paint all surfaces on the play center.

Patio Chair

You won't believe how comfortable plastic tubes can be until you sit in this unique patio chair. It's attractive, reliable and very inexpensive to build.

For solid service, you can't go wrong with our patio chair. Crashing painfully to the ground just when you're trying to relax and enjoy the outdoors is nobody's idea of fun, so we designed this patio chair for durability and comfort. Our patio chair utilizes rigid plastic tubing for cool, comfortable support that's sure to last through many fun-filled seasons. Say good-bye to expensive or highly-specialized patio furniture with this outdoor workhorse.

This inventive seating project features CPVC plastic tubes that function like slats for the back and seat assemblies. The ½"-dia. tubes have just the right amount of flex and support, and can be purchased at any local hardware store. Even though the tubing is light, there is no danger of this chair blowing away in the wind. It has a heavy, solid frame that will withstand strong gusts of wind and fearsome summer showers. For even greater comfort, you can throw a favorite pillow, pad or blanket over the tubing and arms and relax in the sun.

The materials for this project are inexpensive. All the parts except the seat support are made from 2 × 4 cedar. The seat support is made from 1 × 3 cedar. For a companion project to this patio chair, see *Gate-Leg Picnic Tray,* pages 44 to 47.

CONSTRUCTION MATERIALS

Quantity	Lumber
3	2 × 4" × 10' cedar
1	1 × 3" × 2' cedar
7	½" × 10' CPVC tubing

OVERALL SIZE:
36" HIGH
26" WIDE
25" LONG

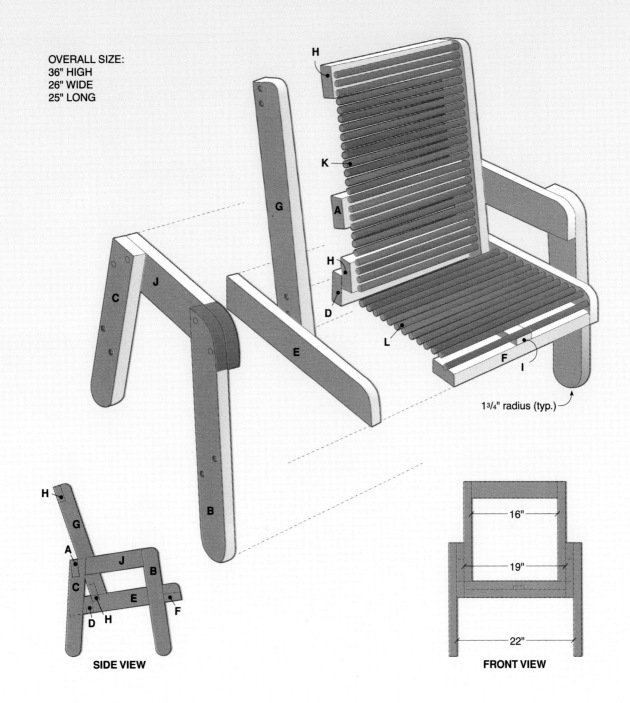

1¾" radius (typ.)

SIDE VIEW

16"

19"

22"

FRONT VIEW

Cutting List					Cutting List				
Key	**Part**	**Dimension**	**Pcs.**	**Material**	**Key**	**Part**	**Dimension**	**Pcs.**	**Material**
A	Back support	1½ × 3½ × 19"	1	Cedar	**G**	Back side	1½ × 3½ × 28"	2	Cedar
B	Front leg	1½ × 3½ × 22½"	2	Cedar	**H**	Back rail	1½ × 3½ × 16"	2	Cedar
C	Rear leg	1½ × 3½ × 20½"	2	Cedar	**I**	Seat support	¾ × 2½ × 17"	1	Cedar
D	Seat stop	1½ × 3½ × 19"	1	Cedar	**J**	Arm rail	1½ × 3½ × 19½"	2	Cedar
E	Seat side	1½" × 3½ × 24½"	2	Cedar	**K**	Back tube	½-dia. × 17½"	25	CPVC
F	Seat front	1½ × 3½ × 19"	1	Cedar	**L**	Seat tube	½-dia. × 20½"	14	CPVC

Materials: Moisture-resistant glue, deck screws (1¼", 2½", 3"), ⅜"-dia. cedar plugs, finishing materials.

Note: Measurements reflect the actual size of dimensional lumber.

Use a portable drilling guide when drilling the holes for the tubes in the seat sides.

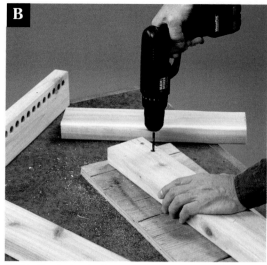

Drill pilot holes before attaching the back rails and sides.

Directions:
Patio Chair

MAKE THE BACK SIDES. The first step in building the patio chair is constructing the back sides. The back sides provide the frame for the CPVC tubing. Make sure all your cuts are accurate and smooth to achieve good, snug-fitting joints. Start by cutting the back sides (G) to length, using a circular saw. Your next step is to drill the stopped holes for the plastic tubes on the inside faces of the back sides. These holes must

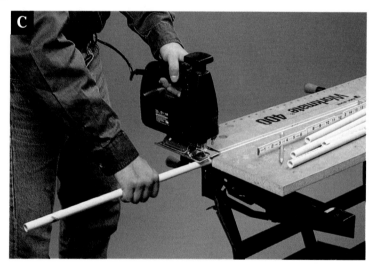

Use a jig saw to cut the CPVC tubing slats. For stability, arrange the tubing so the saw blade is very close to the worksurface.

be accurately positioned and drilled, so use a pencil with either a combination square or a straightedge to draw a centering line to mark the locations for the holes. Make the centering line ⅝" from the front edge of each back side. Drill ⅝-dia. × ¾"-deep holes, and center them exactly 1" apart along the centerline. Start the first hole 3" from the bottom end

of each back side. Use a portable drilling guide and a square to make sure the holes are straight and perfectly aligned **(photo A).** A portable drilling guide fits easily onto your power drill to ensure quick and accurate drilling. Some portable drilling guides are even equipped with depth stops, making them the next best thing to a standard drill press.

BUILD THE BACK FRAME. Once the back sides have been cut and drilled, you can build

the back frame. Start by using a circular saw to cut the back rails (H) to size. These pieces will be attached to the inside faces of the back sides, flush with the back, top and bottom edges. To eliminate the sharp edges, clamp the pieces to a stable worksurface and use a sander or a router to soften the edges on the top and bottom of the back rails, and the top edges of the back sides. Dry-fit the back rails and back sides, and mark their positions with a

Attach the remaining side to complete the back assembly.

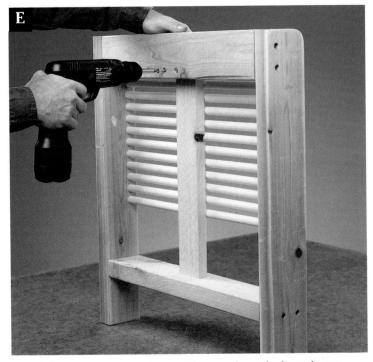

Attach the seat support to the seat front and seat lock as shown.

is usually available in 10' lengths. Use a jig saw to cut 25 pieces of the ½"-dia. CPVC tubing. Remember, these pieces will be used for the back seat assembly only; the seat assembly requires additional pieces. Cut the pieces to 17½" lengths **(photo C).** When you buy plastic tubing, you will find ink grade stamps imprinted on it every several inches along the outside. To make the patio chair more attractive, wash these grade stamps off with lacquer thinner. Always wear gloves and work in a well-ventilated area when using dangerous chemicals, like lacquer thinner. When the grade stamps have been removed, rinse the pipes with water. Once the pipes are clean and dry, insert them one-by-one into the holes on one of the back sides. Slide the remaining back side into place, positioning the plastic tubes into the holes. Fasten the back side to the side rails with glue and counterbored 3" deck screws **(photo D).**

BUILD THE SEAT FRAME. We designed and built the seat frame in much the same way as the back frame. One important difference is in the positioning of the CPVC tubing. On the seat frame, one tube is inserted into

pencil. Bore two ⅜"-dia. × ½"-deep holes into the outside faces of each back side. Make these holes where the back rails will be located. Drill ³⁄₁₆"-dia. pilot holes through the center of each hole **(photo B).** Apply moisture-resistant glue to one end of each rail and fasten them to a single back side with 3" deck screws.

COMPLETE THE BACK ASSEMBLY. Before you start assembling the back, you need to purchase and prepare the CPVC tubing for the frame holes. Make sure the tubing is ½"-dia. CPVC, which is rated for hot water. Standard PVC tubing is not usually sold in small diameters that will fit into the ⅝"-dia. holes you have drilled. This plastic tubing the sides slightly out of line to make the chair more comfortable for your legs. Start by cutting the seat sides (E), seat front (F), seat stop (D) and seat support (I). Use the same methods as with the back frame to draw the centering line for the plastic tubing. Drill the tube holes into each seat side. Start the holes 2" from the front end of the seat sides. Position a single tube hole on the seat frame ⅞" below the top edge, and 1" from the front end of each seat side. This front tube provides a gradual downward seat profile for increased leg comfort when you are seated. To eliminate the sharp edges on the seat assembly, round over the seat sides, seat support edges and seat front edges with a sander or router. Use a combination square to mark a line across the width of the inside of the seat sides, 3½" from the back edges. This is where the seat stop is positioned. Test-fit the pieces to make sure their positions are correct, then lay out and mark the position of the seat stop and seat front on each seat side. Carefully drill pilot holes in position to fasten one seat side, seat support and seat front as you did with the back rails. Connect the parts with moisture-resistant glue and deck screws.

Make identical radius cuts on the bottoms of the legs.

Use a square to make sure the seat is perpendicular to the leg.

COMPLETE THE SEAT FRAME. To complete the seat frame, you must attach the remaining seat side and fasten the seat support to the seat front and seat stop. The seat support (I) is located directly under the plastic tubing in the center of the seat and provides strength and support to the entire seat frame. Begin by cutting 14 pieces of ½"-dia. CPVC pipe. Each piece should be 20½" long. Once again, clean the grade stamps off the tubes with lacquer thinner, rinse them with clean water, and insert them into the holes on one seat side. Carefully slide the remaining seat side into place and fasten the pieces with moisture-resistant glue and deck screws. Attach the seat support to the middle of the seat front and seat stop with moisture-resistant glue and 1¼" deck screws **(photo E)**.

BUILD THE ARMS & LEGS. With the back and seat frames already constructed, the arms and legs are all that remain for

Slide the back frame into the seat frame so the back sides rest against the seat stop and seat support.

the patio chair assembly. When you make the radius cuts on the bottom edges of the front and back legs, make sure the cuts are exactly the same on each leg (see *Diagram*, page 39). Otherwise, the legs may be uneven and rock back and forth when you sit down. Start by cutting the back support (A) and arm rails (J) to size. Fasten the back support between the arm rails with counterbored deck screws and glue. Be sure the back support is flush with the ends of the rails. Cut the front legs (B) and rear legs (C). Use a jig saw to cut a full radius on the bottoms of the legs **(photo F).** Attach the front legs

to the outside of the arm rails so the legs are flush with the ends. It is very important to keep the front legs perpendicular to the arm rails.

ATTACH THE SEAT FRAMES. Attach the leg/arm rail assembly to the seat so that the top edge of the seat frame is 15" from the bottom of the leg. It is important to measure and mark accurately. Remember to position the front of the seat so that it extends exactly 3½" past the leg. Use a square to make sure the seat is perpendicular to the legs **(photo G).** Use glue and screws to fasten the rear legs to the arm rail and seat · side so that the back edge of the leg is flush with the ends of the arm rail and seat side. Trim

the excess material above the arm rail. More than any other, this part of the chair contacts your body, so make sure to round over and sand all the rough edges until they are completely smooth to the touch.

ATTACH THE BACK FRAME. Carefully slide the back frame into the seat frame so that the back sides rest against the seat stop **(photo H).** Make sure the back support and bottom of the back sides are flush with the bottom of the seat sides. Apply moisture-resistant glue, and attach the back frame by driving counterbored deck screws through the seat stop into the back rail.

APPLY THE FINISHING TOUCHES. For a fine decorative touch, apply glue to the bottoms of ⅜"-dia. cedar wood plugs, and insert them into the screw counterbores. Sand the tops of the plugs until they are even with the surrounding surface. Wipe the wood surfaces with a rag dipped in mineral spirits, then apply finishing materials. We used a clear wood sealer on the patio chair to preserve the look of the cedar.

TIP

When making the radius cuts on the bottom edges of the legs remember that when using a jig saw, it is tempting to speed up a cut by pushing the tool with too much force. Jig saw blades have a tendency to bend during curves, causing irregular cuts and burns. Since cedar is vulnerable to burning, be sure to make steady cutting passes. Curved cuts are easiest to make with multiple passes. Once the cuts have been made, sand the cut surfaces smooth.

Gate-Leg Picnic Tray

Make outdoor dining on your porch, patio or deck a trouble-free activity with our picnic tray. Built with gate legs, it provides a stable surface for plates or glasses, yet folds up easily for convenient storage.

PROJECT
POWER TOOLS

Outdoor dining doesn't need to be a messy, shaky experience. Whether you're on the lawn or patio, you can depend on our gate-leg picnic tray. A hinged leg assembly allows you to fold the tray for easy carrying and storage. Two of the legs are fastened directly to supports beneath the main tray surface with hinges, while the third is attached only to the other legs, allowing it to swing back and forth like a gate and aid compact storage. A small wedge fits under the tray to prevent the swinging leg from moving once the tray is set up.

Our picnic tray also features a hinged bottom shelf that swings down and locks in place with a hook-and-eye clasp to keep the legs in place. Of course, the most conspicuous feature of the project is the tray surface. Plastic tubing is a durable material, and it makes cleaning the tray top easy. The tubing also gives the project an interesting look—it's a companion piece to the patio chair on pages 38-43. Use a portable drill and drill stand to make the holes in the tray sides and insert the plastic tubing. CPVC tubing is a relatively lightweight material, but the strong cedar frame gives our project more stability than you'll get in conventional folding trays.

Even on grass, our gate-leg picnic tray will serve you well, allowing you to enjoy your meal without fear of a messy, dinnertime disaster.

CONSTRUCTION MATERIALS

Quantity	Lumber
1	1 × 2" × 12' cedar
1	1 × 3" × 6' cedar
1	1 × 4" × 8' cedar
1	1 × 12" × 2' cedar
4	½" × 10' CPVC tubing

OVERALL SIZE:
18" WIDE
22³/₈" HIGH
19" LONG

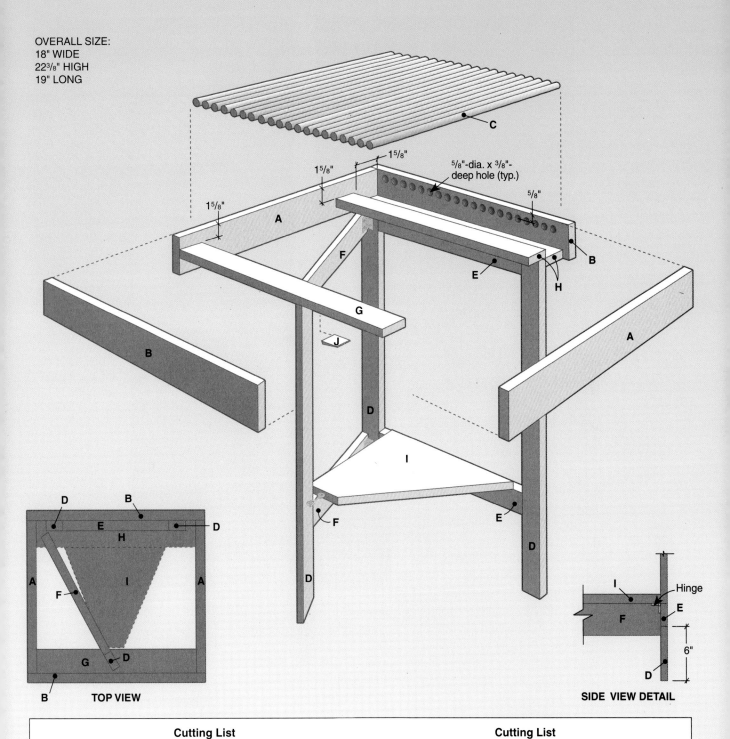

⁵/₈"-dia. x ³/₈"-deep hole (typ.)

1⁵/₈"

TOP VIEW

SIDE VIEW DETAIL

6"

Hinge

Cutting List				
Key	Part	Dimension	Pcs.	Material
A	Side	³/₄ × 3½ × 16½"	2	Cedar
B	Cap	³/₄ × 3½ × 19"	2	Cedar
C	Tube	⁵/₈"-dia. × 17¼"	20	CPVC
D	Leg	³/₄ × 1½ × 20"	3	Cedar
E	Short rail	³/₄ × 2½ × 13"	2	Cedar

Cutting List				
Key	Part	Dimension	Pcs.	Material
F	Long rail	³/₄ × 1½ × 13½"	2	Cedar
G	Gate support	³/₄ × 2½ × 17½"	1	Cedar
H	Hinge support	³/₄ × 1½ × 17½"	2	Cedar
I	Shelf	1 × 10 × 12¾"	1	Cedar
J	Wedge	¼ × 2 × 2"	1	Cedar

Materials: Moisture-resistant glue, deck screws (1¼", 1½", 2", 3"), wire brads, exterior wood putty, hinges, finishing materials.

Note: Measurements reflect the actual size of dimensional lumber.

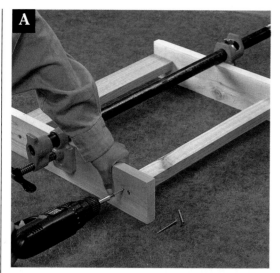

*Clamp the pieces to hold them in place, and at-
tach the hinge support 1⅝" from the top side edge.*

*Once the final cap has been attached with deck
screws and glue, the basic tray frame is complete.*

Directions:
Gate-Leg Picnic Tray

MAKE THE TRAY FRAME. First,
construct the upper section of
the project. It's a simple frame
with stopped holes cut into the
caps for the CPVC tubing. The
underside of the tray frame is
braced by supports, which
provide a surface on which to
anchor the legs. Begin by cutting the sides (A) and caps (B)
to length from 1 × 4 cedar. Use
a power drill to make ⅝ × ⅜"-
deep holes for CPVC tubing, 1"
apart in the inside faces of the
caps. We recommend using a
portable drill stand for this step
(see *Tip*, below). Start the holes
1½" from one end and center

*Attach the rails
to the legs with
counterbored
deck screws
and glue.*

the holes ⅝" from the top cap
edges. Cut the gate support (G)
from 1 × 3 cedar and cut the
hinge supports (H) from 1 × 2
cedar. Drill two evenly spaced
¼ × ⅜"-dia. counterbored holes
into the outside face of the
front end of each of the sides,
where the gate support will be
attached. Drill the holes 1⅝"
down from the top edges of the
sides. Apply moisture-resistant
glue to the joints and clamp the
piece with a bar clamp. Drill
³⁄₁₆"-dia. pilot holes through
each center, then fasten the

gate support to the sides with
2" deck screws. On the opposite side of the frame, fasten
one hinge support between the
sides **(photo A).** Make sure the
hinge support is fastened 1⅝"
from the ends of the sides, and
1⅝" from the top side edges.
Fasten one of the caps to the
side assembly with deck
screws.

CUT & INSTALL THE TUBES. Use
a jig saw or compound miter
saw to cut 24 pieces of ½"-dia.
CPVC tubing (C) to 17¼" in
length. For more information
on working with plastic tubing,
see *Patio Table*, page 38-43.

Attach the leg frames with high-quality hinges.

Fasten the stationary leg frame to the lower hinge support on the underside of the tray frame.

Use wire brads and glue to attach the lock wedge, which holds the gate leg assembly in place.

Wash the grade stamps from the tubing with lacquer thinner and rinse them with clean water. When the tubes are dry, insert the them into their holes in the frame. Fasten the remaining cap to the frame with glue and deck screws **(photo B).** Next, attach the remaining hinge support to the sides, starting ⅞" from the end on the outside edge. This hinge support should be flush with the bottom edges of the sides. Use glue and countersunk deck screws to attach the pieces.

BUILD THE LEG ASSEMBLY. The leg assembly consists of two leg frames and a series of rails. One leg frame is stationary and is attached to the bottom hinge support with hinges. The other frame has only one leg, which swings like a gate and is attached only to the first frame. These braces are attached to the other leg frame. Begin the leg assembly by cutting the legs (D), short rails (E), and long rails (F) from 1 × 2 cedar. Fasten the rails to the legs (see *Diagram,* page 45) with counter-bored deck screws and glue to form two leg frames **(photo C).** The bottom edge of the rails should be 4" from the bottom

of the legs. The top rails should be flush with the top leg edges. Attach the gate leg frame to the stationary frame with hinges **(photo D),** then fasten the stationary legs to the bottom hinge support **(photo E).** To prevent the gate leg from swinging back and collapsing the assembled picnic tray, cut a lock wedge from 1 × 3 cedar. Open the gate leg to the normal standing position, which should be roughly the center of the gate support. Draw a line on the gate support along the edge of the gate leg to locate the wedge position. Use wire brads and glue to attach the lock wedge so that its thin end is against the gate leg **(photo F).** The leg will slide over this wedge slightly and be held fast. Cut the shelf (K) to size and shape. Attach it to the short rails with hinges. Install a hook-and-eye clasp on the gate leg and shelf to secure the open assembly. Sand all sharp edges and finish the project with clear wood sealer.

TIP

Use cedar plugs to fill the counter-bores for the screws in the tray frame.

Front-porch Mailbox

This cedar mailbox is a practical, good-looking project that is very easy to build. The simple design is created using basic joinery and mostly straight cuts.

PROJECT
POWER TOOLS

If you want to build a useful, long-lasting item in just a few hours, our mailbox is the project for you. Replace that impersonal metal mailbox you bought at the hardware store with a distinctive cedar mailbox that is a lot of fun to build. The lines and design are so simple on this project that it suits nearly any home entrance. Our mailbox features a hinged lid and a convenient lower shelf that is sized to hold magazines and newspapers.

We used select cedar to build our mailbox, then applied a clear, protective finish. Plain brass house numbers dress up the flat surface of the lid, which also features a decorative scallop that doubles as a handgrip.

If you are ambitious and economy-minded, you can build this entire mailbox using just one 8'-long piece of 1 × 10 cedar. That means, however, that you will have to do quite a bit of rip-cutting to make the parts. If you have a good straightedge and some patience, rip-cutting is not difficult. But you may prefer to simply purchase dimensional lumber that matches the widths of the pieces (see the *Construction Materials* list to the left).

If your house is sided with wood siding, you can hang the mailbox by screwing the back directly to the siding. If you have vinyl or metal siding, be sure that the screws make it all the way through the siding and into wood sheathing or wood wall studs. If you have masonry siding, like brick or stucco, use masonry anchors to hang the mailbox.

CONSTRUCTION MATERIALS

Quantity	Lumber
1	1 × 10" × 4' cedar
1	1 × 8" × 4' cedar
1	1 × 4" × 3' cedar
1	1 × 3" × 3' cedar
1	1 × 2" × 3' cedar

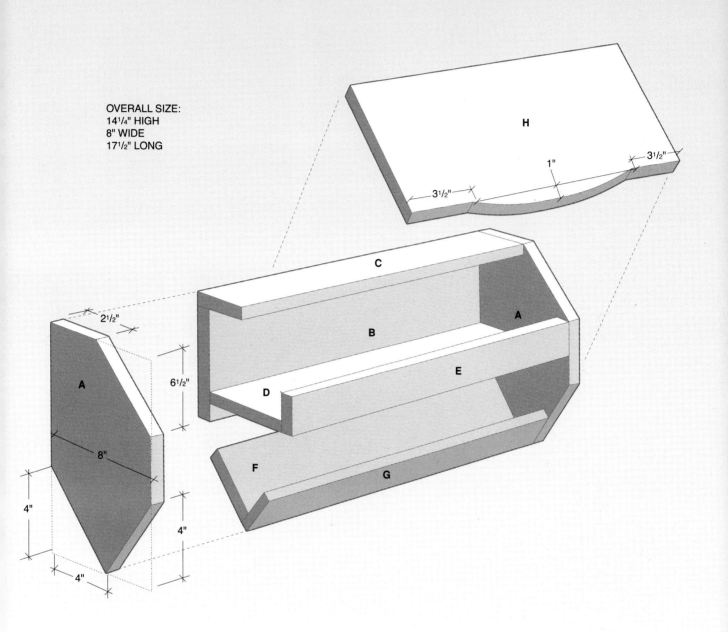

OVERALL SIZE:
14¼" HIGH
8" WIDE
17½" LONG

Cutting List				
Key	Part	Dimension	Pcs.	Material
A	Side	¾ × 8 × 14¼"	2	Cedar
B	Back	¾ × 7¼ × 16"	1	Cedar
C	Top	¾ × 2½ × 16"	1	Cedar
D	Box bottom	¾ × 6½ × 16"	1	Cedar

Cutting List				
Key	Part	Dimension	Pcs.	Material
E	Box front	¾ × 1½ × 16"	1	Cedar
F	Shelf bottom	¾ × 3½ × 16"	1	Cedar
G	Shelf lip	¾ × 2½ × 16"	1	Cedar
H	Lid	¾ × 9¼ × 17½"	1	Cedar

Materials: Moisture-resistant wood glue, 2" deck screws, masking tape, continuous hinge, finishing materials.

Note: Measurements reflect the actual size of dimensional lumber.

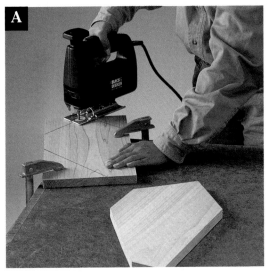

Cutlines are drawn on the sides, and the parts are cut to shape with a jig saw.

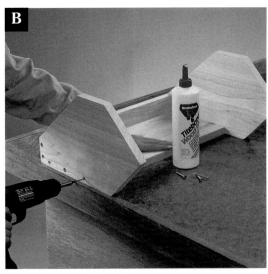

After fastening the top between the sides, fasten the back with deck screws.

Directions:
Front-porch Mailbox

BUILD THE SIDES. The sides are the trickiest parts to build in this mailbox design. But if you can use a ruler and cut a straight line, you should have no problems. First, cut two 8 × 14¼" pieces of ¾"-thick cedar to make the sides (A)—pieces of wood that will be shaped into parts are called "blanks" in the woodworkers' language. Next, lay out the cutting pattern onto one side blank, using the measurements shown on page 49. Mark all of the cutting lines, then double-check the dimensions to make sure the piece will be the right size when it is cut to shape. Make the cuts in the blank, using a jig saw, to create one side. Sand the edges smooth. Now, use the

Attach the bottom to the back with glue and screws driven through the back and sides.

side as a template to mark the second blank (this ensures that the two sides are identical). Try to arrange the template so the grain direction is the same in the blank and the template. Cut out and sand the second side **(photo A).**

ATTACH THE BACK & TOP. Use 2" deck screws and exterior wood glue to fasten all the pieces on the mailbox. Although cedar is a fine outdoor wood, it can be quite brittle, so drill pilot holes to prevent splitting the cedar edges, and space

the screws evenly when driving them into the pieces. Begin by cutting the back (B) and top (C) to size. Fasten the top between the 2½"-wide faces on the two sides. using glue and 2" deck screws. Position the top so that the rear face is flush with the rear side edges, and the top face is flush with the top side edges. Use glue and deck screws to fasten the back between the sides, flush with

Keep the lip edges flush with the side edges to form the newspaper shelf.

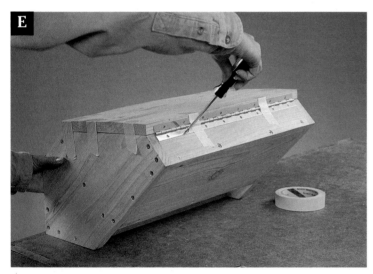

Once the pieces are taped in place, the continuous hinge is attached to join the lid to the top.

the 8"-long edges **(photo B),** and butted against the top.

ATTACH THE BOX BOTTOM & FRONT. Once assembled, the bottom and front pieces form the letter compartment inside the mailbox. Start by cutting the bottom (D) and front (E). Fasten the bottom to the back and sides, making sure the bottom edges are flush **(photo C).** Once the bottom is attached, fasten the front to the sides and bottom, keeping the bottom edges flush.

ATTACH THE NEWSPAPER SHELF. The lower shelf on the underside of the mailbox is designed for overflow mail, especially magazines and newspapers. To make the lower shelf, cut the shelf bottom (F) and shelf lip (G) to size. Fasten the shelf bottom to the leg of the "V" formed by the sides that is closer to the back. Fasten the shelf lip to the sides along the front edges to complete the shelf assembly **(photo D).**

CUT & ATTACH THE LID. Begin by cutting the lid (H) to size (9¼" is the actual width of a 1 × 10). Draw a reference line parallel to and 1" away from one of the long edges. Use a jig saw to make a 3½"-long cut at each end of the line. Mark the midpoint of the edge (8¾"), then cut a shallow scallop to connect the cuts with the midpoint. Smooth out the cut with a sander. Attach a brass, 15"-long continuous hinge (sometimes called a "piano hinge") to the top edge of the lid. Then position the lid so the other wing of the hinge fits squarely onto the top of the mailbox. Secure the lid to the mailbox with masking tape, then attach the hinge to the mailbox **(photo E).**

APPLY THE FINISHING TOUCHES. Sand all the surfaces until they are completely smooth with 150-grit sandpaper, then finish the mailbox as desired. We used clear wood sealer. We also added 3" brass house numbers on the lid, but you may prefer to stencil an address or name onto the lid (see *Tip*, page 50). Once the finish has dried, hang the mailbox on the wall by driving screws through the back (see page 50).

TIP

Clear wood sealer can be refreshed if it starts to yellow or peel. Wash the wood with a strong detergent, then sand the surface lightly to remove flaking or peeling sealer. Wash the surface again, then simply brush a fresh coat of sealer onto the wood.

Sun Lounger

Designed for the dedicated sun worshipper, this sun lounger has a backrest that can be set in either a flat or an upright position.

CONSTRUCTION MATERIALS

Quantity	Lumber
3	2 × 2" × 8' pine
1	2 × 4" × 8' pine
5	2 × 4" × 10' pine
2	2 × 6" × 10' pine

Leave your thin beach towel and flimsy plastic chaise lounge behind as you relax and soak up the sun in this solid wood sun lounger. Set the adjustable backrest in an upright position while you make your way through your summer reading list. Then, for a change of pace, set the backrest in the flat position and drift off in a pleasant reverie. If you are an ambitious suntanner, take comfort in the fact that this sun lounger is lightweight enough that it can be moved easily to follow the path of direct sunlight. Made almost entirely from inexpensive pine or cedar, this sun lounger can be built for only a few dollars—plus a little sweat equity.

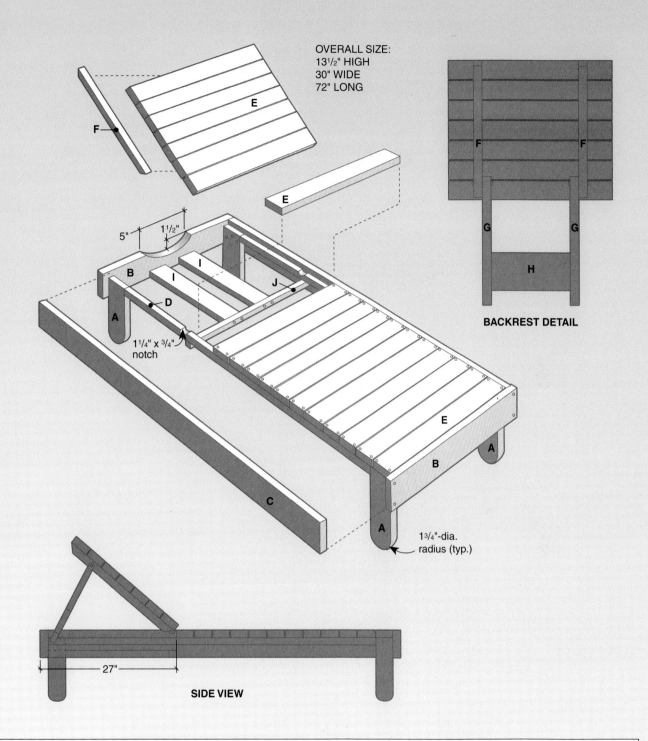

OVERALL SIZE:
13½" HIGH
30" WIDE
72" LONG

BACKREST DETAIL

5"   1½"

1¼" x ¾"
notch

1¾"-dia.
radius (typ.)

27"

SIDE VIEW

Key	Part	Dimension	Pcs.	Material
A	Leg	1½ × 3½ × 12"	4	Pine
B	Frame end	1½ × 5½ × 30"	2	Pine
C	Frame side	1½ × 5½ × 69"	2	Pine
D	Ledger	1½ × 1½ × 62"	2	Pine
E	Slat	1½ × 3½ × 27"	19	Pine

Key	Part	Dimension	Pcs.	Material
F	Back brace	1½ × 1½ × 22"	2	Pine
G	Back support	1½ × 1½ × 20"	2	Pine
H	Cross brace	1½ × 5½ × 13"	1	Pine
I	Slide support	1½ × 3½ × 24"	2	Pine
J	Slide brace	1½ × 1½ × 27"	1	Pine

Materials: Moisture-resistant wood glue, 2½" deck screws, (2) ¼"-dia. × 3½" carriage bolts with washers and nuts.

Note: Measurements reflect the actual size of dimensional lumber.

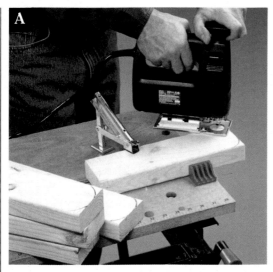

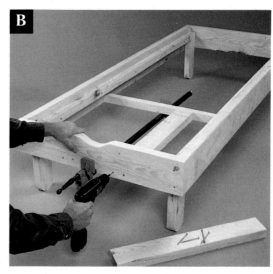

Use a jig saw to cut roundovers on the bottoms of the legs.

Assemble the frame pieces and legs, then add the support boards for the slats and backrest.

Use ⅛"-thick spacers to keep an even gap between slats as you fasten them to the back braces and the ledgers in the bed frame.

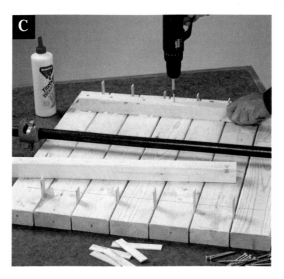

Directions: Sun Lounger

MAKE THE LEGS. Start by cutting the legs (A) to length from 2 × 4 pine. To ensure uniform length, cut four 2 × 4s to about 13" in length, then clamp them together edge to edge and gang-cut them to final length (12") with a circular saw. Use a compass to scribe a 3½"-radius roundoff cut at the bottom corners of each leg. Make the roundoff cuts with a jig saw **(photo A),** then sand smooth. The rounded leg bottoms help the sun lounger rest firmly on uneven surfaces.

CUT THE FRAME PIECES & LEDGERS. Cut the frame ends (B) and frame sides (C) from 2 × 6 pine. Use a jig saw to cut a 5"-wide, 1½"-deep arc into the top edge of one frame end, centered end to end, to create a handgrip. Cut the ledgers (D) from 2 × 2 pine. Measure 24"

from one end of each ledger and place a mark, then cut a 1¼"-wide, ¾"-deep notch into the top edge of each ledger, centered on the 24" mark. Smooth out the notch with a 1½"-radius drum sander mounted on a power drill (this notch will serve as the pivot for the back support). Sand all parts and smooth out all sharp edges.

ASSEMBLE THE FRAME. The lounge frame consists of the legs, the side and end frame pieces, and the long ledger strips that support the slats. Begin assembly by attaching the frame sides and frame ends to form a box around the legs, with the tops of the frame pieces 1½" above the tops of the legs to leave space for the 2 × 4 slats. Use glue and 2¼" deck screws, driven from the inside of the frame. Attach the ledgers to the frame sides, fitted between the legs, using glue and 2" deck screws. Make sure the ledger tops are flush with the tops of the legs, and the notches are at the same end as the notch in the frame.

TIP

For a better appearance, always keep the screws aligned. In some cases, you may want to add some screws for purely decorative purposes: in this project, we drove 1" deck screws into the backrest slats to continue the lines created by the screw heads in the lower lounge slats.

CUT & INSTALL THE BACKREST SUPPORTS. Cut the slide brace (J) from 2 × 2 pine. Position the slide brace between the frame sides, 24" from the notched frame end, fitted against the bottom edges of the ledgers. Glue and screw the slide brace to the bottom edges of the ledgers. Cut the slide supports (I) to length from 2 × 4 pine, then position the supports so they are about 3" apart, centered below the notch in the frame end. The ends of the supports should fit neatly against the frame end and the slide brace. Attach with glue and screws driven through the frame end and the slide brace, and into the ends of the slide supports **(photo B).**

FASTEN THE SLATS. Start by cutting all the slats (E) for the project to length from 2 × 4 pine. Use a straightedge guide to ensure straight cuts (the ends will be highly visible), or simply hold a speed square against the edges of the boards and run your circular saw along the edge of the speed square. Cut the back braces (F) from 2 × 2 pine. Lay seven of the slats on a flat worksurface, and slip ⅛"-wide spacers between the slats. With the ends of the slats flush, set the back braces onto the faces of the slats, 4" in from the ends. Drive a 2" deck screw through the brace and into each slat **(photo C).** Install the remaining slats in the bed frame, spaced ⅛" apart, by driving two screws through each slat end and into the tops of the ledgers. One end slat should be ⅛" from the inside of the uncut frame end, and the other 27" from the outside of the notched frame end.

ASSEMBLE THE BACKREST SUPPORT FRAMEWORK. The adjustable backrest is held in place by a small framework that is attached to the back braces. The framework can either be laid flat so the backrest also lies flat, or raised up and fitted against the inside of the notched frame end to support the backrest in an upright position. Cut the back supports (G) from 2 × 2 pine, then clamp the pieces together face to face, with the ends flush. Clamp a belt sander to your worksurface, and use it as a grinder to round off the supports on one end. Cut the cross brace (H) to length from 2 × 6 pine. Position the cross brace between the back supports, 2" from the non-rounded ends, and attach with glue and 2½" deck screws driven through the cross brace and into the edges of the supports. Next, position the rounded ends of the supports so they fit between the ends of the back braces, overlapping by 2½" when laid flat. Drill a ¼"-dia. guide hole through the braces and the supports at each overlap joint. Thread ¼"-dia. × 3"-long carriage bolts through the guide holes, with a flat washer between each support and brace. Hand-tighten a washer and nylon locking nut onto each bolt end (see **photo D** for a view of how these parts fit together).

INSTALL THE BACKREST. Set the backrest onto the ledger boards near the notched end of the frame. With the backrest raised, tighten the locking nut on the backrest support framework until it is tight enough to hold the framework together securely, while still allowing the joint to pivot **(photo D).**

APPLY THE FINISHING TOUCHES. Sand all surfaces and edges **(photo E)** to eliminate the possibility of slivers. After sanding, we applied two coats of water-based, exterior polyurethane for a smooth, protective finish. You may prefer to use light-colored exterior paint.

Use a washer and nylon locking nut to fasten the back braces to the back supports.

Sand all surfaces carefully to eliminate splinters, and check to make sure all screw heads are set below the wood surface.

Outdoor Occasional Table

*The traditional design of this deck table provides a stylishly simple
addition to any porch, deck or patio.*

CONSTRUCTION MATERIALS	
Quantity	**Lumber**
2	1 × 3" × 8' cedar
6	1 × 4" × 8' cedar

Create a functional yet stylish accent to your porch, deck or patio with this cedar deck table. This table makes an ideal surface for serving cold lemonade on hot summer days, a handy place to set your plate during a family cookout, or simply a comfortable place to rest your feet after a long day. Don't be fooled by its lightweight design and streamlined features; this little table is extremely sturdy. Structural features such as middle and end stringers tie the aprons and legs together and transfer weight from the table slats to the legs. This attractive little table is easy to build and will provide many years of durable service.

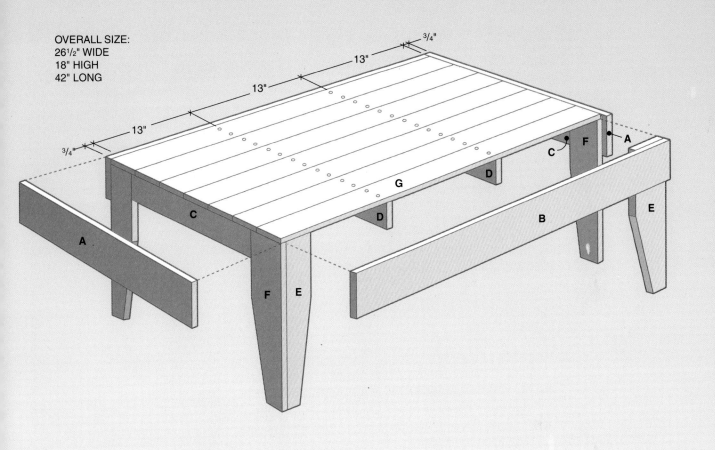

OVERALL SIZE:
26½" WIDE
18" HIGH
42" LONG

Cutting List				
Key	**Part**	**Dimension**	**Pcs.**	**Material**
A	End apron	¾ × 3½ × 26½"	2	Cedar
B	Side apron	¾ × 3½ × 40½"	2	Cedar
C	End stringer	¾ × 2½ × 18"	2	Cedar
D	Middle stringer	¾ × 2½ × 25"	2	Cedar

Cutting List				
Key	**Part**	**Dimension**	**Pcs.**	**Material**
E	Narrow leg side	¾ × 2½ × 17¼"	4	Cedar
F	Wide leg side	¾ × 3½ × 17¼"	4	Cedar
G	Slat	¾ × 3½ × 40½"	7	Cedar

Materials: Moisture-resistant glue, 1¼" deck screws.

Note: Measurements reflect the actual size of dimensional lumber.

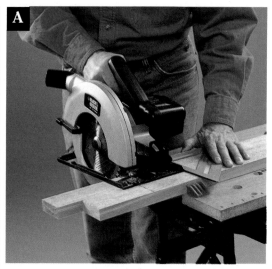

Use a speed square as a cutting guide and gang-cut the table parts when possible for uniform results.

Mark the ends of the tapers on the leg sides, then connect the marks to make taper cutting lines.

Directions: Outdoor Occasional Table

MAKE THE STRINGERS & APRONS. The stringers and aprons form a frame for the tabletop slats. To make them, cut the end aprons (A) and side aprons (B) from 1 × 4 cedar **(photo A).** For fast, straight cutting, use a speed square as a saw guide—the flange on the speed square hooks over the edge of the boards to hold it securely in place while you cut. Cut the end stringers (C) and middle stringers (D) from 1 × 3 cedar.

MAKE THE LEG PARTS. Cut the narrow leg sides (E) to length from 1 × 3 cedar. Cut the wide leg sides (F) to length from 1 × 4 cedar. On one wide leg side piece, measure 8¾" along one edge of leg side and place a mark. Measure across the bottom end of the leg side 1½" and place a

TIP

Rip-cut cedar 1 × 4s to 2½" in width if you are unable to find good clear cedar 1 × 3s (nominal). When rip-cutting, always use a straightedge guide for your circular saw. A straight piece of lumber clamped to your workpiece makes an adequate guide, or buy a metal straightedge guide with built-in clamps.

Use a jig saw or circular saw to cut the leg tapers.

mark. Connect the two marks to create a cutting line for the leg taper. Mark cutting lines for the tapers on all four wide leg sides **(photo B).** On the thin leg sides, measure 8¾" along an edge and ¾" across the bottom end to make endpoints for the taper cutting lines. Clamp each leg side to your worksurface, and cut along the taper cutoff line, using a jig saw or circular saw, to create the tapered leg sides **(photo C).** Sand all of the leg parts until smooth.

ASSEMBLE THE LEG PAIRS. Apply a ½"-wide layer of moisture-resistant glue on the face of a wide leg side, next to the untapered edge. Then apply a thin layer of glue to the untapered edge of a narrow leg side. Join the leg sides together at a right angle to form a leg pair. Reinforce the joint with 1¼" deck screws. Glue and screw the rest of the leg pairs in the same manner **(photo D).** Be careful not to use too much glue: it can get messy and also will cause problems later if you

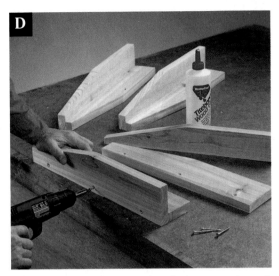

Fasten the leg pairs by driving deck screws through the face of the wide side and into the narrow edge.

Test the layout of the slats before you fasten them, adjusting as necessary to make sure gaps are even.

plan to stain or clear-coat the finish.

MAKE THE TABLETOP FRAME. Now fasten the side aprons (B) to the leg pairs with glue and screws. Be sure to screw from the back side of the leg pair and into the side aprons so the screw heads will be concealed. The narrow leg side of each pair should be facing in toward the center of the side apron, with the outside faces of the wide leg sides flush with the ends of the side apron. The tops of the leg pairs should be ¾" down from the tops of the side aprons to create recesses for the tabletop slats. Now attach the end aprons (A) to the leg assemblies. Use glue, and drive screws from the back side of the leg pairs. Make sure the end aprons are positioned so the ends are flush with the outside faces of the side aprons. Once the aprons are fastened to the pairs, attach the end stringers (C) to the end aprons between the leg pairs. Use glue, and drive the screws from the back sides of the end stringers

and into the end aprons. Cut the middle stringers (D) to length, then measure 13" in from the inside face of each end stringer and mark reference lines on the side aprons for positioning the middle stringers (see page 57). Attach the middle stringers to the side aprons, centered on the reference lines, using glue and deck screws driven through the side aprons and into the ends of the middle stringers. Make sure the middle stringers are positioned ¾" down from the tops of the side aprons.

CUT AND INSTALL THE SLATS. Before you start cutting the slats (G), measure the inside dimension between the end aprons to be sure that the slat length is correct. Once you've confirmed the length, cut the slats to length from 1 × 4 cedar, using a circular saw and a speed square to keep the cuts square. It is extremely important to make square cuts on the ends of the slats because they are going to be the most visible cuts on the entire table. Once all the slats are cut, run a bead of glue along the top faces of

the middle and end stringers. Screw the slats to the stringers leaving a gap of approximately ¹⁄₁₆" between each of the individual slats **(photo E)**.

APPLY THE FINISHING TOUCHES. Smooth all sharp edges by using a router with a roundover bit or a power sander with medium-grit (#100 to 120) sandpaper. Finish-sand the entire table, clean off the sanding residue and apply your finish. We used clear wood sealer. We left the screw heads exposed, but if you prefer, you can fill the screw counterbores with tinted wood putty.

TIP

Clamp all workpiece parts whenever possible during the assembly process. Clamping will hold glued-up and squared-up parts securely in place until you permanently fasten them with screws. Large, awkward assemblies will be more manageable with the help of a few clamps.

Planters

These cedar planters are simple projects that can transform a plain plant container into an attractive outdoor accessory.

CONSTRUCTION MATERIALS

Quantity	Lumber
1	1 × 10" × 6' cedar
1	¼ × 20 × 20" hardboard or plywood

Add a decorative touch to your deck, porch or patio with these stylish cedar planters. Created using square pieces of cedar fashioned together in different design patterns, the styles shown above feature circular cutouts that are sized to hold a standard 24-ounce coffee can. To build them, simply cut 1 × 10 cedar to 9¼" lengths, then make 7¼"-diameter cutouts in the components as necessary. We used a router and template to make the cutouts with production speed. Follow the assembly instructions (see page 63 and the diagrams on page 61) to create the three designs above. Or, you can create your own designs by rearranging the components or altering the cutout size.

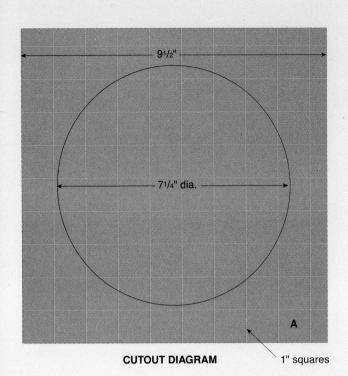

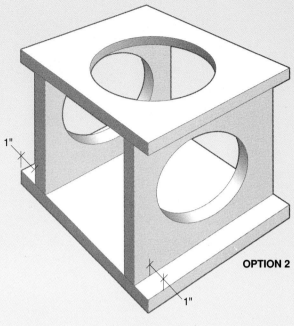

CUTOUT DIAGRAM

9½"

7¼" dia.

A

1" squares

1"

1"

OPTION 2

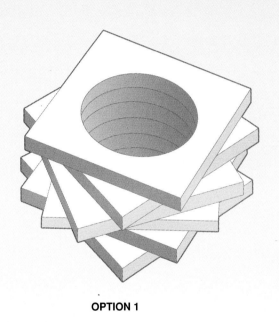

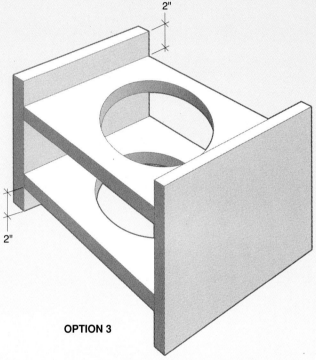

2"

2"

OPTION 1

OPTION 3

Cutting List				
Key	**Part**	**Dimension**	**Pcs.**	**Material**
A	Component	¾ × 9¼ × 9¼"	*	Cedar

Materials: Moisture-resistant glue, 2" deck screws, 24-ounce coffee can, finishing materials.

* Number of pieces varies according to planter style.

Note: Measurements reflect the actual size of dimensional lumber.

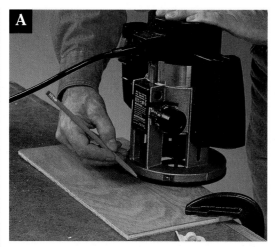

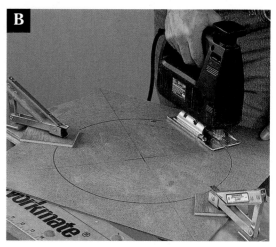

Outline the router base onto scrap material to help determine the router-base radius.

Cut out the router template using a jig saw.

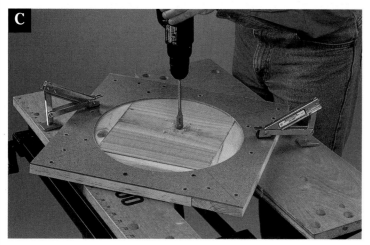

Drill a starter hole for the router bit in the centers of the components.

Directions: Planters

MAKE THE ROUTER TEMPLATE. Using a router and a router template is an excellent method for doing production style work with uniform results. To create the cutout components for our planters, we made a circular template to use as a cutting guide for the router. Determining the size of the template circle is simple: just add the radius of your router base to the radius of your fin-

TIP

Plunge routers are routers with a bit chuck that can be raised or lowered to start internal cuts. If you own a plunge router, use it to cut parts for this project. Otherwise, drill a starter hole as shown, for a standard router.

ished cutout (3⅝" in the project as shown). Begin by finding the radius of your router base: first, install a 1"-long straight bit in your router (for fast cutting, use a ¾"-diameter bit, but make sure you use the same bit for making the template and cutting the components); make a shallow cut into the edge of a piece of scrap wood; then, with the router bit stopped, trace around the outside edge of the router base with a pencil **(photo A).** Measure from the perimeter of the router cut to the router-base outline to find the radius. Add 3⅝" for the radius of a 24-ounce coffee can

and, using a compass, draw a circle with this measurement onto the template material. Cut out the router template using a jig saw **(photo B).**

MAKE THE PARTS. The planters are built from identical components (A) of 1 × 10 cedar. Cut the number of components required for your design to length, then make circular cutouts on those components that require them. To make a circular cutout, start by drawing diagonal lines connecting the corners of the component. The point of intersection is the center of the square board. Center the template on the component, and clamp it in place. Use a drill to bore a 1"-diameter starter hole for the router bit (unless you are using a plunge router—see *Tip,* left) at the center **(photo C).** Position the router bit inside the hole. Turn the router on and move it away from the starter hole until the router base contacts the template. Pull the router in a counterclockwise direction around the inside of the template to make the cutout. Smooth any sharp edges with sandpaper.

OPTION 1

Assembly Options

Option 1. Attach the pieces on the stacked planter from top to bottom, ending with a solid base. To make this stacked planter, you need six pieces of 1 × 10 cedar. Cut them to length, and rout circular shapes in five of them. The solid piece will be the base. Stack the pieces on top of the base component. Place a painted coffee can in the center and arrange the sections to achieve a spiralling effect (see Diagram, page 61). Use a pencil to mark the locations of the pieces. Remove the can and fasten the pieces together using glue and deck screws. Attach the pieces by driving the deck screws through the lower pieces into the upper pieces, fastening the base last.

OPTION 2

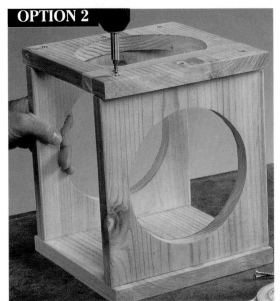

Option 2. Use four components on this option to create a planter with three cutout components and a solid base. Measure and mark lines 1" from each side edge on the solid component and one of the cut-out components. Attach the inner components with their inside faces flush with these lines. Fasten the solid component to the sides with moisture-resistant glue and deck screws, then attach the remaining cut-out component to finish the planter. Insert a painted coffee can.

OPTION 3

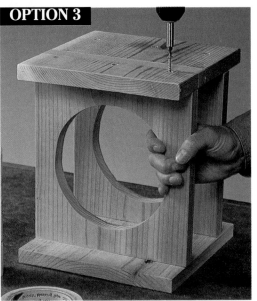

Option 3. Attach two components with circular cutouts to the inside faces of two solid components to make this planter. Measure and mark guidelines 2" from the top and bottom edges on the two solid components. Fasten the two cut-out components between the others with moisture-resistant glue and deck screws, making sure their outside edges are flush with the drawn guidelines. Insert a painted coffee can.

Adirondack Chair

You will find dozens of patterns and plans for building popular Adirondack chairs in just about any bookstore, but few are simpler to make than this clever project.

Adirondack furniture has become a standard on decks, porches and patios throughout the world. It's no mystery why this distinctive furniture style has become so popular. The straightforward design, expansive surfaces, and the unmatched stability are just a few of the reasons, and our Adirondack chair offers all of these benefits, and more. But unlike most of the Adirondack chairs you may find, this chair is also very easy to build. There are no complex compound angles to cut, no intricate details on the back and seat slats, and no mortise-and-tenon joints. Like all projects in this book, our Adirondack chair can be built by any do-it-yourselfer, using basic tools and simple techniques. But because this design features all the elements that make an Adirondack chair an Adirondack chair, your guests and neighbors may never guess that you built it yourself.

We made our Adirondack chair out of cedar and finished it with clear wood sealer. But you may prefer to build your version from pine (a traditional wood type for Adirondack furniture), especially if you plan to paint the chair. White, battleship gray and forest green are common colors for Adirondack furniture. Be sure to use quality exterior paint with a glossy or enamel finish.

CONSTRUCTION MATERIALS

Quantity	Lumber
1	2 × 6" × 8' cedar
1	2 × 4" × 10' cedar
1	1 × 6" × 14' cedar
1	1 × 4" × 12' cedar
1	1 × 2" × 8' cedar

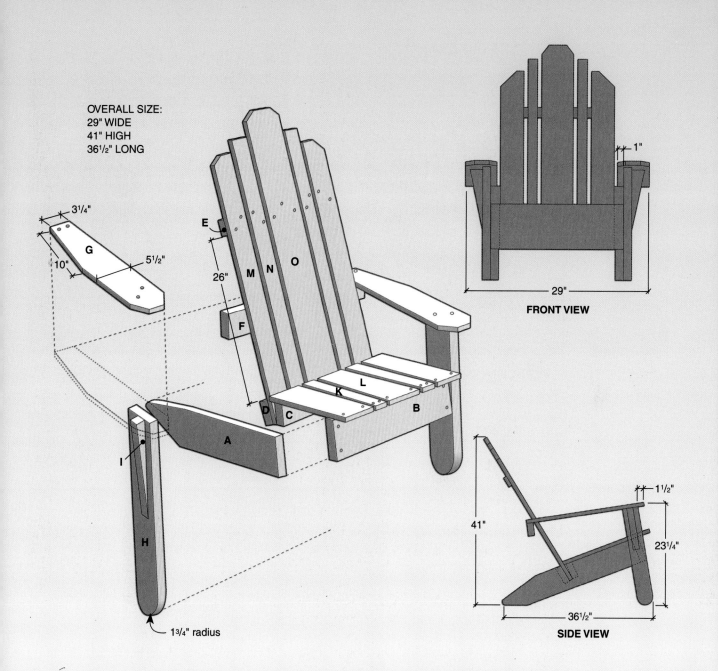

OVERALL SIZE:
29" WIDE
41" HIGH
36½" LONG

FRONT VIEW

SIDE VIEW

1¾" radius

Cutting List

Key	Part	Dimension	Pcs.	Material
A	Leg	1½ × 5½ × 34½"	2	Cedar
B	Front	1½ × 5½ × 21"	1	Cedar
C	Seat support	1½ × 3½ × 18"	1	Cedar
D	Low back brace	1½ × 3½ × 18"	1	Cedar
E	High back brace	¾ × 3½ × 18"	1	Cedar
F	Arm cleat	1½ × 3½ × 24"	1	Cedar
G	Arm	¾ × 5½ × 28"	2	Cedar
H	Post	1½ × 3½ × 22"	2	Cedar

Cutting List

Key	Part	Dimension	Pcs.	Material
I	Arm brace	1½ × 2¼ × 10"	2	Cedar
K	Narrow seat slat	¾ × 1½ × 20"	2	Cedar
L	Center seat slat	¾ × 5½ × 20"	3	Cedar
M	End back slat	¾ × 3½ × 36"	2	Cedar
N	Narrow back slat	¾ × 1½ × 38"	2	Cedar
O	Center back slat	¾ × 5½ × 40"	1	Cedar

Materials: Moisture-resistant glue, deck screws (1¼", 1½", 2", 3"), ⅜ × 2½" lag screws with washers, finishing materials.

Note: Measurements reflect the actual size of dimensional lumber.

Cut tapers into the back edges of the legs.

Round over the sharp slat edges with a router or power sander.

Directions: Adirondack Chair

CUT THE LEGS. Wide, sprawling back legs that support the seat slats and stretch to the ground on a near-horizontal plane are telltale features of Adirondack style. To make the legs (A), first cut two 34½"-long pieces of 2 × 6. Mark the tapers onto the back end of one board. First, mark a point on the end of the board, 2" from the edge. Then mark another point on the edge, 6" from the end. Connect the points with a straightedge. Then, mark another point on the same end, 2¼" in from the other edge. Mark a point on that edge, 10" from the end. Connect these points to make a cutting line for the other taper. Make the two taper cuts with a circular saw, then use the leg as a template for marking identical tapers on the other leg board. Cut the second leg **(photo A).**

Make decorative cuts on the fronts of the arms (shown) and the tops of the back slats, using a jig saw.

BUILD THE SEAT. The legs form the sides of the box frame that supports the seat slats. Cut the front apron (B) and seat support (C) to size. Attach the apron to the front ends of the legs with glue and 3" deck screws driven through counterbored pilot holes. For the 3" deck screws used throughout most of this project, drill ⅛"-dia. pilot holes through ⅜"-dia. × ¼"-deep counterbores, then insert ⅜"-dia. cedar plugs into the counterbores when assembly is finished. Position the seat support so the inside face is 16½" from the inside edge of the front apron. Attach the seat support between the legs, making sure the tops of the part are flush.

D

Attach the square ends of the posts to the undersides of the arms, being careful to position the part correctly.

Next, cut the seat slats (K) and (L) to length from 1 × 2 and 1 × 6, respectively, and sand the ends smooth. Arrange the slats on top of the seat box (see page 65), with ⅜" spaces between slats—use wood scraps as spacers. The slats should overhang the front of the seat box by ¾". Fasten the seat slats by driving counterbored 2" deck screws through the ends of the slats and into the top of the front apron and the seat support in back. Be careful to keep the counterbores aligned so the cedar plugs form straight lines across the front and back of the seat. Once all the slats are installed, use a router with a ¼" round-over bit (or a power sander) to smooth the edges and ends of the slats **(photo B).**

MAKE THE BACK SLATS. Like the seat slats, the back slats in our design are made from three sizes of dimension lumber (1 × 4, 1 × 2, and 1 × 6). Cut the back slats (M), (N), (O), to size. For a decorative touch

that is simple to create, we trimmed off corners on the wider slats. On the 1 × 6 slat (O), mark points 1" in from the outside, top corners of the slat, then mark points on the outside edges, 1" down from the corners. Connect the points, then trim off the corners with a jig saw, following the lines. Mark the 1 × 4 slats 2" from one top corner, in both directions. Draw cutting lines, then trim off these corners.

ATTACH BACK SLATS TO BRACE. Cut the low back brace (D) and high back brace (E). Set the braces on a flat worksurface, then slip ¾"-thick spacers under the high brace so the top is level with the low brace. Arrange the back slats on top of the braces with

the same pattern and spacing used with the seat slats. The untrimmed ends of the slats should be flush with the bottom edge of the low back brace, and the bottom of the high back brace should be 26" above the top of the low brace. Use ¾" spacers to set gaps and make sure the braces are exactly perpendicular to the slats. Attach the slats to the low brace with counterbored 2" deck screws, and to the high brace with 1¼" deck screws (see page 65 for a suggested screw pattern).

CUT THE ARMS. The broad arms of this Adirondack chair are supported by posts in front, and a cleat that is attached to the backs of the chair slats. Start by cutting the arms (G) to size. For decoration, cut a triangle with 1½"-long sides from the front corners of each arm, using a jig saw or circular saw **(photo C).** Then, make a tapered cut on the inside, back edge of each arm. Mark points for the cut onto the back end of each arm, 3¼" in from each inside edge. Mark the outside edges 10" from the back, connect the points, then cut the tapers with a circular saw or jig saw. Sand all edges smooth.

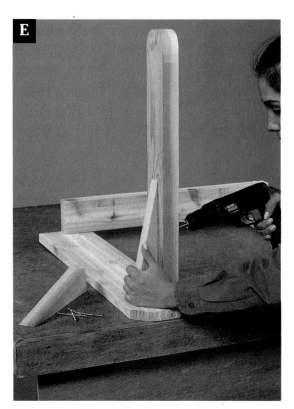

E

F

Drive screws through each post and into the top of an arm brace to stabilize the arm/post joint.

Clamp wood braces to the parts of the chair to hold them in position while you fasten the parts together.

ASSEMBLE THE ARMS, CLEATS & POSTS. Cut the arm cleat (F) and make a mark 2½" in from each end. Set the cleat on edge on your worksurface. Position the arms on the top edge of the cleat so the back ends of the arms are flush with the back of the cleat and the untapered edge of each arm is aligned with the 2½" mark. Fasten the arms to the cleats using glue and counterbored 3" deck screws. Cut the posts (H) to size, then use a compass to mark a 1¾" radius roundover cut on each bottom post cor-

ner (the rounded bottoms make the Adirondack chair more stable on uneven surfaces). Position the arms on top of the square ends of the posts, with the faces of the post parallel to the sides of the arms. The posts should be set back 1½" from the front ends of the arm, and 1" from the inside edge of the arm. Fasten the arms to the posts with glue and counterbored 3" deck screws **(photo D).** Cut tapered arm braces (I) from wood scraps, making sure the grain of the wood runs lengthwise (see page 65). Position an arm brace at the outside of each arm/post joint, centered side to side on the post. Attach each brace with glue and 2" counterbored deck screws driven through the inside face of the

post and into the brace, near the top **(photo E).** Also drive a 2" deck screw down through each arm and into the top of the brace.

ASSEMBLE THE CHAIR. All that remains is to join the back, seat/leg assembly and arm/post assembly to complete the construction of the Adirondack chair. Before you start, gather up some scrap pieces of wood to use to help brace the parts while you fasten them together. First, set the seat/leg assembly onto your worksurface, clamping a piece of scrap wood to the front apron to raise the front of the assembly until the bottoms of the legs are flush on the surface (about 10"). Use a similar technique to brace the arm/post assembly so the bottom of the back cleat is 20" above the worksurface. Arrange the arm/post assembly so the posts fit around the front

TIP

Making tapered cuts with a circular is not difficult if the alignment marks on your saw base are accurate. Before attempting to make a tapered cut where you enter the wood at an angle, always make test cuts on scrap wood to be sure the blade starts cutting in alignment with the alignment marks on your saw. If not, either re-set your alignment marks, or compensate for the difference when you cut the tapers.

of the seat/leg assembly, with the bottom edge of the apron flush with the front edges of the posts. Drill a ¼"-dia. pilot hole through the inside of each leg and partway into the post. Drive a ⅜ × 2½"-long lag screw (with washer) through each pilot hole, but do not tighten completely in case you need to make any assembly adjustments **(photo F).** Remove the braces. Now, slide the back into position so the low back brace is between the legs, and the slats are resting against the front of the arm cleat. Clamp the back to the seat support with a C-clamp, making sure the top of the low brace is flush with the tops of the legs where they meet. Use a square to check to see that the ends of the seat slats meet the front faces of the back slats at a right angle. If not, adjust the relative position of the assemblies until a right angle is achieved. Fully tighten the lag screws at the post/leg joints, then add a second lag screw at each joint. Finally, drive three evenly spaced 1½" deck screws through counterbored pilot holes (near the top edge of the arm cleat) and into the back slats to secure the back **(photo G).** Also drive 3" screws through the legs and into the ends of the lower back brace.

APPLY FINISHING TOUCHES. Glue ¼"-thick, ⅜"-dia. cedar wood plugs into all the visible screw counterbores **(photo H).** After the glue dries, sand the plugs level with the surrounding surface, then finish-sand all the exposed surfaces with 120-grit sandpaper. Finish as desired—we simply applied a coat of clear wood sealer.

Drive screws through the arm cleat, near the top and into the slats.

Glue cedar plugs into counterbores to conceal the screw holes.

Boot Butler

*A traditional piece of home furniture, the boot butler combines
shoe storage and seating in one dependable unit.*

CONSTRUCTION MATERIALS

Quantity	Lumber
1	¾" × 4 × 8' plywood
2	4" × 4' pine ranch molding

Our boot butler was designed for an enclosed front porch, but it can be used near any household entrance. It provides plenty of storage space and gives you a solid seat when you're putting on or removing your shoes and boots. This boot butler is a classic piece of household furniture that we modernized and simplified for your home. Just fit some plastic boot trays neatly onto the bottom shelf to keep mud from making a filthy mess on the carpet. When the trays get dirty, simply take them out and clean them. The boot butler can handle the footwear of the entire family, and it fits conveniently against the wall to save space and keep unsightly boots and shoes out of busy traffic lanes.

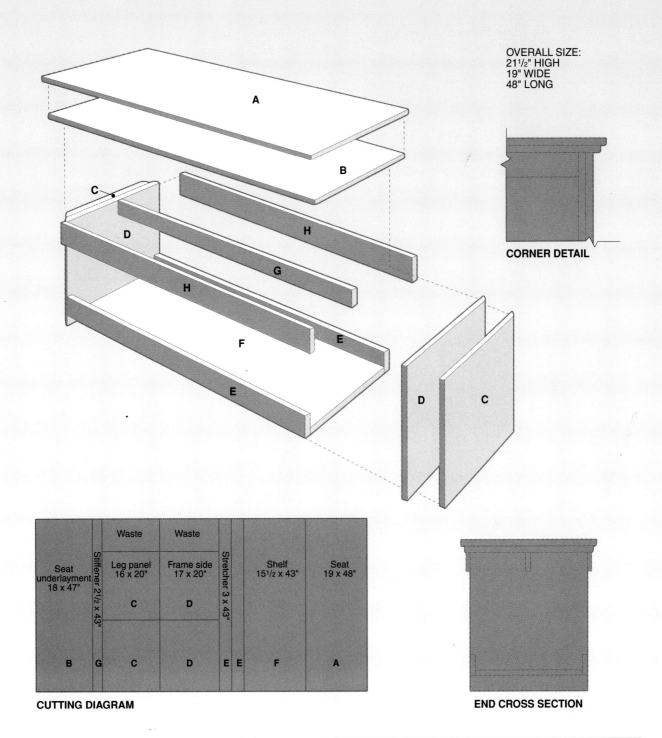

OVERALL SIZE:
21½" HIGH
19" WIDE
48" LONG

CORNER DETAIL

CUTTING DIAGRAM

Seat underlayment 18 x 47"

Stiffener 2½ x 43"

Waste — Leg panel 16 x 20" — C

Waste — Frame side 17 x 20" — D

Stretcher 3 x 43"

Shelf 15½ x 43"

Seat 19 x 48"

B G C D E E F A

END CROSS SECTION

Cutting List

Key	Part	Dimension	Pcs.	Material
A	Seat	¾ × 19 × 48"	1	Plywood
B	Underlayment	¾ × 18 × 47"	1	Plywood
C	Leg panel	¾ × 16 × 20"	2	Plywood
D	Frame side	¾ × 17 × 20"	2	Plywood

Cutting List

Key	Part	Dimension	Pcs.	Material
E	Stretcher	¾ × 3 × 43"	2	Plywood
F	Shelf	¾ × 15½ × 43"	1	Plywood
G	Stiffener	¾ × 2½ × 43"	1	Plywood
H	Apron	½ × 3½ × 43¾"	2	Pine

Materials: Moisture-resistant glue, deck screws (1¼", 2"), 8d finish nails, 15 × 21" plastic boot trays, finishing materials.

Note: Measurements reflect the actual size of dimensional lumber.

Directions: Boot Butler

CUT THE PLYWOOD PARTS. Cut all of the following parts with a circular saw and straightedge (refer to the *Cutting Diagram* on page 71 to see how to lay out and cut all the parts from one sheet of plywood): seat (A), seat underlayment (B), leg panel (C), frame side (D), stretchers (E), shelf (F) and stiffener (G). Smooth out the sides of the legs, the top edges of the stretchers, and all the edges of the seat and underlayment with a sander or a router and ¼" roundover bit.

Use glue to reinforce the joints between the stretchers and the shelf.

ASSEMBLE THE SHELF & STRETCHERS. All the plywood parts are connected with screws and glue. Before you drive the screws, drill counterbores for the screw heads that are just deep enough to be filled with wood filler or putty. Attach the stretchers and shelf by drilling four evenly spaced ³⁄₁₆"-dia. pilot holes through the outside edges of the stretchers and into the front and back edges of the shelf. Keep the screw holes at least 2" from the ends of the stretchers to prevent splitting when you drive the screws. Glue the joints **(photo A),** and drive 2" deck screws through the pilot holes and into the shelf.

BUILD THE BOX FRAME. Now, attach the two frame sides (D) to the ends of the shelf assembly. To accomplish this, mark the location of the parts onto the frame sides. Begin by measuring and marking a line 2" up from the bottom edge of each frame side. This is where the lower edges of the stretchers will fit when the stretchers are installed. The stiffener (G) is positioned between the frame sides, at the top, center points

to provide stability to the box frame. Mark the stiffener position, making sure the top of the stiffener is flush with the tops of the frame sides, and apply glue to all the joints. Clamp the stretchers and stiffener in position with bar clamps. Drill two evenly spaced ³⁄₁₆"-dia. pilot holes through each frame side and into the ends of the stiffener. Drive the 2" deck screws to secure the stiffener **(photo B).** For extra shelf support, drill pilot holes and drive a screw through the center of each frame side into the shelf.

COMPLETE THE LEG ASSEMBLY. Attach leg panels (C) to the outer faces of the frame sides to provide wider, more stable support points for the seat. Put wax paper or newspaper on your work surface to catch any excess glue, then apply glue to the outer face of each frame side, and to the inner face of each leg panel. Press the leg panels against the frame panels, centered side to side to create a ½" reveal on each side of each frame panel. All top and bottom edges should be flush. Clamp each panel pair together **(photo C),** then secure with

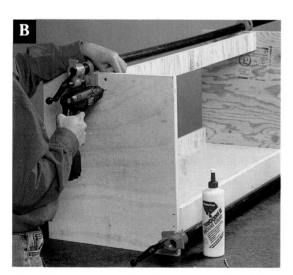

The stiffener is screwed in place between the sides to keep the boot butler square.

A pair of plywood panels are fastened together to create each leg assembly.

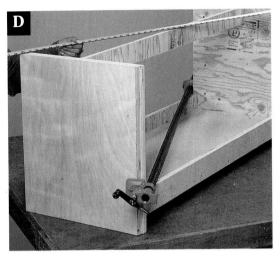

If the frame isn't square, fasten a pipe clamp diagonally across it and tighten.

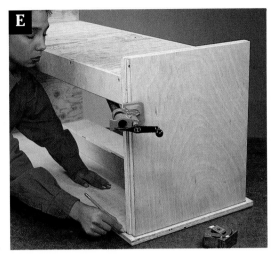

Set the frame assembly onto the underlayment. Center and trace the outline on the underlayment.

counterbored 1¼" deck screws driven through the frame panels into the leg sides. Check the box frame to make sure it is square by measuring diagonally from corner to corner, across the tops of the leg assembly. Use a pipe clamp to draw the frame together until it is pulled into square, and the diagonal measurements are equal **(photo D).**

ATTACH THE SEAT ASSEMBLY. The seat for the boot butler is made up of two sheets of plywood: a ¾"-thick underlayment (B) layered together with the plywood seat (A). Lay the underlayment on a flat surface, then flip the leg and shelf assembly upside-down and center it on the bottom face of the underlayment. Outline the edges of the frame onto the underlayment for future reference **(photo E).** Flip the leg and shelf assembly upright, and apply glue to the tops of the legs and stiffener. Position the underlayment on the assembly according to the alignment marks. Drill ³⁄₁₆"-dia. counterbored pilot holes through the underlayment into the legs and stiffeners, then

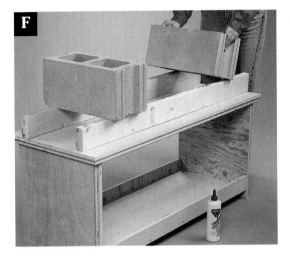

Apply weight on the seat to ensure a solid glue bond with the seat underlayment.

drive 2" deck screws. Apply a thin layer of glue to the top of the underlayment and the underside of the seat. Position the seat onto the underlayment so the overhang is the same on all sides. Set heavy weights on top of the seat to help create a solid glue bond **(photo F).** Drive evenly spaced, counterbored 1¼" deck screws through the underlayment into the seat. Finally, cut the aprons (H) from 4"-wide pine ranch molding. Position the aprons so the tops are flush against the bottom edges of the underlayment, overlapping the edges of the frame panels slightly. Attach with 8d finish nails.

APPLY FINISHING TOUCHES. Fill all of the countersunk screw holes and plywood edges with wood putty and sand smooth. Apply primer and paint—we painted our boot butler with cream-colored exterior latex enamel paint. For a decorative touch, stencil or sponge-paint the surfaces.

TIP

Rigid, clear plastic boot trays are sold at most discount stores or building centers. The Boot Butler project shown here is designed to hold 15 × 21" plastic boot trays.

Bird Feeder

A leftover piece of cedar lap siding is put to good use in this rustic bird feeder.

CONSTRUCTION MATERIALS

Quantity	Lumber
1	¾ × 16 × 16" plywood scrap
1	¾" × 6' cedar stop molding
1	8" × 10' cedar lap siding
1	1 × 2" × 8' cedar
1	1"-dia. × 3' dowel

Watching birds feeding in your backyard can be a very relaxing pastime. In this bird feeder project, we used a piece of 8"-wide cedar lap siding to build the decorative feeder box that is mounted on a piece of scrap plywood. The birds didn't seem to mind the left-over building materials, and we were excited because the bird feeder cost almost nothing to build. Even the plastic viewing window covers inside the feeder box were made from a small scrap of clear acrylic left over from another project. To fill this cleverly designed bird feeder, just turn the threaded rod that serves as a hook so it is aligned with the slot in the roof. Then, lift up the roof and add the bird food.

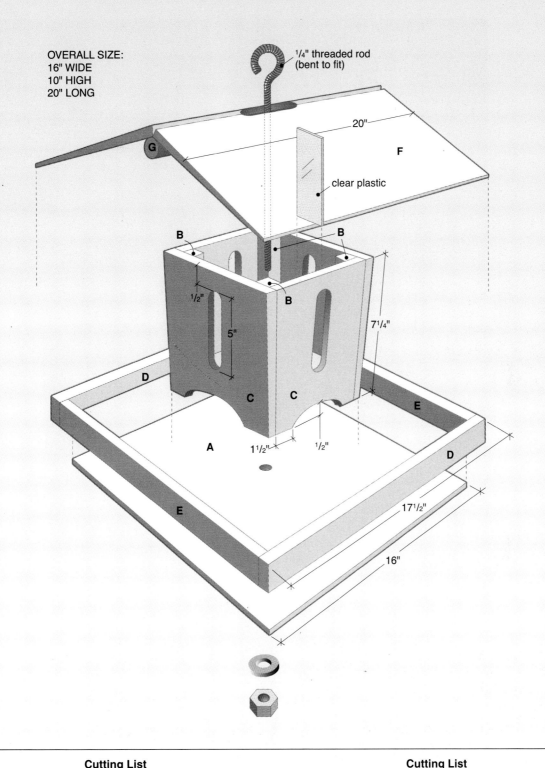

OVERALL SIZE:
16" WIDE
10" HIGH
20" LONG

¼" threaded rod
(bent to fit)

20"

F

clear plastic

B

B

B

½"

5"

7¼"

D

C

C

E

A

1½"

½"

E

D

17½"

16"

Cutting List

Key	Part	Dimension	Pcs.	Material
A	Base	¾ × 16 × 16"	1	Plywood
B	Post	¾ × ¾ × 7¼"	4	Cedar
C	Box side	⁵⁄₁₆ × 6 × 7¼"	4	Cedar siding
D	Ledge side	¾ × 1½ × 17½"	2	Cedar

Cutting List

Key	Part	Dimension	Pcs.	Material
E	Ledge end	¾ × 1½ × 16"	2	Cedar
F	Roof panel	⁵⁄₁₆ × 7¼ × 20"	2	Cedar siding
G	Ridge pole	1"-dia. × 20"	1	Dowel

Materials: ¼"-dia. threaded rod with matching nut and washer, wood glue, hotmelt glue, 4d common nails, rigid acrylic or plastic.

Note: Measurements reflect the actual size of dimensional lumber.

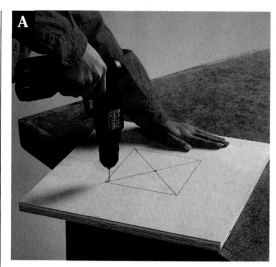

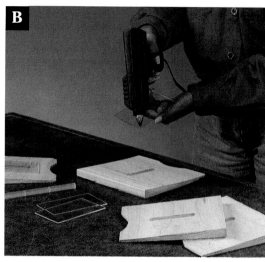

Drill pilot holes at the corners of the feeder box location that is laid out on the plywood base.

Cover the viewing slots by hot-gluing clear plastic or acrylic pieces to the inside face of each panel.

Directions: Bird Feeder

CUT & PREPARE THE BASE. Cut the plywood base (A) from ¾"-thick plywood. Draw straight diagonal lines from corner to corner to locate the center of the square base. Measure and mark a 6" square in the middle of the base, making sure the lines are parallel to the edges of the base. This square shows the eventual location of the feeder box. Drill a ¼"-dia. hole through the center of the base where the lines cross. Measure in toward the center ⅜" from each corner of the 6" square and mark points. Drill 1/16"-dia. pilot holes all the way through the base at these points **(photo A).**

PREPARE THE FEEDER BOX PARTS. The posts and box sides form the walls of the feeder box. Vertical grooves in the box sides create viewing windows so you can check the food level. Small arcs cut in the bottoms of the box sides allow the

Mark the profile of the bevel of the siding onto two of the box sides for trimming.

food to flow through to the feeding area in a controlled fashion. To build the feeder box, cut the posts (B) to size from ¾"-square cedar stop molding (if you prefer, you can rip a 3'-long piece of ¾"-thick cedar to ¾" in width to make the posts). From 8" cedar lap siding (actual dimension is 7¼") cut two 6"-wide box sides (C). Then cut two more panels to about 7" in width; these will be trimmed to follow the lap-siding bevels. Now, cut a viewing slot in each box side. First, drill two ½"-dia. starter holes for

a jig saw blade along the center of each box side—make one hole 2" from the top, and the other 2" from the bottom. Connect the starter holes by cutting with a jig saw to cut the slots. Also cut a ½"-deep arc into the bottom of each box side, using the jig saw. Start the cuts 1½" from each end. Smooth out the arcs with a drum sander mounted on a power drill. Finally, cut strips of clear acrylic or plastic slightly larger than the viewing slots. Hot-glue the strips behind the slots on the inside faces of the box sides **(photo B).** To mark cutting lines for trimming two of the

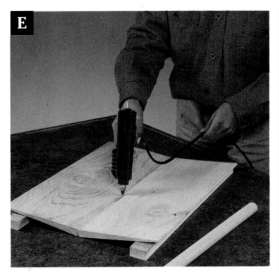

Drive 4d common nails through pilot holes to fasten the feeder box to the base.

Insert spacers 2" in from the "eaves" of the roof to set the pitch before applying glue to the seam.

box sides to follow the siding bevel, tape the box side together into a box shape. The wide ends of the beveled siding should all be flush. Trace the siding profile onto the the inside faces of the two box ends **(photo C)**. Disassemble the box, then cut along the profile lines with a jig saw.

ASSEMBLE THE FEEDER BOX. Start the assembly by hot-gluing the posts flush with the inside edges on the box sides that are trimmed to follow the bevel profile. Then complete the assembly by hot-gluing the untrimmed box sides to posts.

ATTACH THE BASE. Align the assembled feeder box with the 6" square drawn on the base. Glue the box to the base on these lines, then turn the entire assembly upside down. Attach the base to the feeder box by driving 4d galvanized common nails through the pre-drilled pilot holes in the base, and into the posts on the feeder box **(photo D)**.

INSTALL THE BASE FRAME. Cut the ledge sides (D) and ledge

ends (E) from 1 × 2 cedar, to build a frame around the base so bird food does not spill out. Attach the ledge pieces so the bottoms are flush with the bottom of the base, using hot glue. Reinforce the joint with 4d common nails.

MAKE THE ROOF. Cut the ridge pole (G) from a 1"-dia. dowel, and cut the roof panels (F) from 8" siding. Lay the panels on your worksurface so the wide ends butt together. Slip a 1"-thick spacer 2" in from each of the narrow ends to create the roof pitch. Apply a heavy bead of hot glue into the seam between panels **(photo E),** then quickly press the ridge pole into the seam before the glue hardens completely. Let the glue harden for at least 15 minutes. Set the roof down (right-side-up) so the ends of the ridge pole each rest on a 2 × 4 block. Drill ⅜"-dia. starter holes through the roof and the ridge pole, 1" on each side of the midpoint of the ridge. Connect the starter holes by cutting with a jig saw. Widen the slot until the ¼"-dia. threaded rod will pass through with only

minimal resistance. Cut the ¼"-dia. threaded rod to 16" in length, then use pliers to bend a 1½"-dia. loop in one end of the rod. Thread the unbent end of the rod through the roof and the hole in the base **(photo F),** then spin the rod loop so it is perpendicular to the roof ridge (preventing it from slipping into the slot). Tighten a washer and nut onto the end of the rod, loosely enough that the loop can be spun with moderate effort. We didn't apply a finish to our bird feeder.

The bird feeder is held together by a looped, threaded rod that runs through the roof and is secured with a washer and nut on the underside of the base.

Porch Rocker

*You don't have to wait until you're retired to enjoy the comfortable
embrace of this sturdy plywood and pine porch rocker.*

CONSTRUCTION MATERIALS

Quantity	Lumber
1	¾" × 4 × 8' plywood
1	1 × 2" × 3' pine
2	1 × 3" × 8' pine
2	1 × 4" × 10' pine
1	1 × 6" × 4' pine

Escape your daily pressures and problems in this comfortable porch rocker. Our unique design incorporates rocker side panels that are easily cut from plywood sheets with a jig saw. Other frame components consist of solid pine dimensional lumber for simplicity of construction. Broad pine armrests are fitted onto the plywood sides and are big enough to hold a glass of lemonade on those hot summer days. The slatted seat and back provide additional comfort and support while the compact design lets our porch rocker fit nicely even in small porches, where space is at a premium.

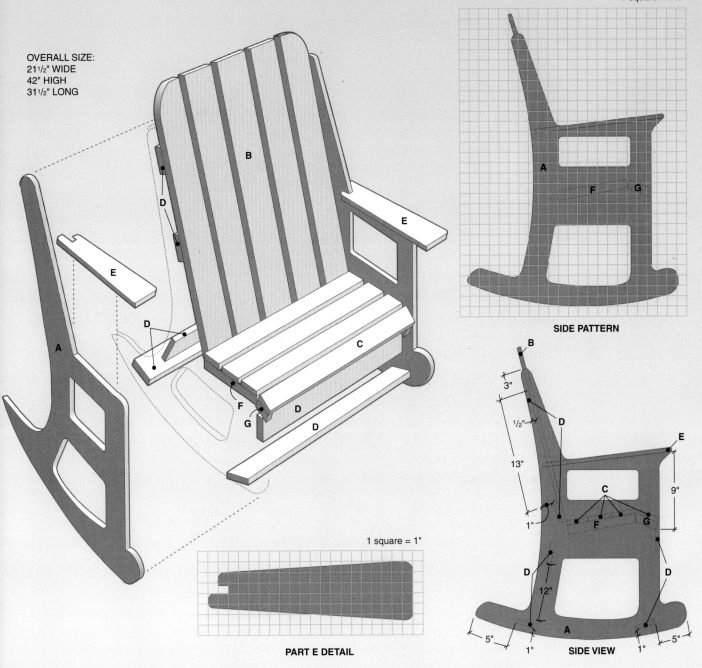

1 square = 1½"

OVERALL SIZE:
21½" WIDE
42" HIGH
31½" LONG

SIDE PATTERN

3"
½"
13"
1"
12"
5"   1"   5"
1"

SIDE VIEW

1 square = 1"

PART E DETAIL

Key	Part	Dimension	Pcs.	Material
A	Sides	¾ × 32 × 39¾"	2	Plywood
B	Back slat	¾ × 3½ × 28"	5	Pine
C	Seat slat	¾ × 3½ × 20"	4	Pine
D	Stretcher	¾ × 2½ × 20"	6	Pine

Cutting List

Key	Part	Dimension	Pcs.	Material
E	Arm	¾ × 5½ × 20"	2	Pine
F	Seat cleat	¾ × 1½ × 8"	2	Pine
G	Front seat cleat	¾ × 1½ × 3"	2	Pine

Materials: Moisture resistant glue, wood screws (#8 × 1¼", #8 × 1½"), finishing materials.

Note: Measurements reflect the actual size of dimensional lumber.

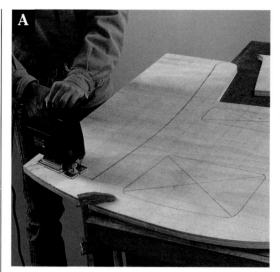

Cut out the rocker sides from 48 × 48" pieces of plywood using a jig saw.

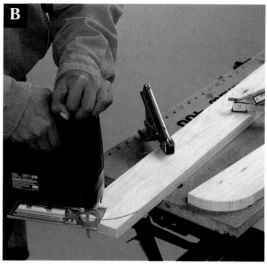

Cut the curved contours at the tops of the outer back slats using a jig saw.

Directions:
Porch Rocker

CREATE THE PLYWOOD SIDES. The sides are cut from 48 × 48" pieces of ¾"-thick plywood. Start by using the porch rocker detail drawing (page 79) to lay out the rocker sides on ¾" plywood. Lay out the side pattern on a 48 × 48" piece of plywood. Make marks at 1½" intervals along all sides, then connect the marks to create a layout grid. Use the side pattern (page 79) as a reference for drawing the side shape onto the plywood. Once the sides are laid out and marked, cut out the rocker sides using a jig saw **(photo A).** For interior cutouts, drill out the corners with a ⅜" bit, then use a jig saw to connect the holes by cutting along the layout lines. Lay the side on another 48 × 48" piece of plywood, trace the design and proceed to cut out the other side. Use a router with a

Clamp the workpiece securely to the workbench when using a router. Align the cutting guide and clamp it in place.

¼" roundover bit or a palm sander to smooth all of the edges, except those edges where the arms will be attached.

CUT THE SLATS, CLEATS AND STRETCHERS. The slats, cleats and stretchers are very simple to make. Start by cutting the back slats (B) to length from 1 × 4 lumber. Lay out a 3"-radius contour on the top ends of the two outside slats using a compass or by simply tracing an appropriately-sized tin can, then cut the curved

contours with a jig saw **(photo B).** Smooth out the jig saw cuts with a belt sander or a drum sander attachment on a drill. Next, cut the seat slats (C) to length from 1 × 4 lumber and the stretchers (D) to length from 1 × 3 lumber. Then cut the seat cleats (F) and (G) to length from 1 × 2 lumber.

MAKE THE ARMS. Making the arms involves cutting tapers and radius corners, and also requires you to cut a groove with

TIP

When using a grid-type pattern, enlarge the pattern on a photocopier so it is as close to actual size as possible to make it easier to transfer to the cutting stock.

a router. Start by cutting two 24"-long pieces of 1 × 6 lumber. Lay out the arms on each piece according to the arm detail diagram (page 79). Then, clamp the pieces to your workbench and, using a router with a straightedge cutting guide and a ¾" straight bit, start at one end and cut a ⅜"-deep, ¾"-wide groove down the center of each arm **(photo C).** Stop the groove cut 1½" from the front edge of the arm, otherwise the groove will be visible from the front of the rocker. Next, cut out the arms along the layout lines. Cut the curved corners with a jig saw and the tapers using a jig saw or circular saw. With a router and a ¼" round-over bit, smooth all of the edges on the arms. Sand all of the edges and surfaces before assembly.

ASSEMBLE THE PORCH ROCKER. The assembly is fairly quick and easy. On the inside surfaces of the plywood sides, lay out the locations of all stretchers according to the detail diagram. Drill pilot holes from the inside out, then on the outside surface, counterbore the pilot holes **(photo D).** Fill the screw holes with wood filler when assembly is complete. Next, lay out the locations for the seat cleats, then glue and screw them in place using #8 × 1¼" wood screws. Drive the screws through the cleats into the rocker sides. Attach the stretchers, using glue and screws, in the designated locations on both rocker sides. Start with the four corner stretchers, then the two remaining stretchers. Attach the seat slats to the seat cleats using glue and wood

screws, again slightly counter-sinking the screws so the holes can be filled with wood filler. Complete the assembly process by attaching the back slats to the stretchers and to the rear seat slats using glue and screws **(photo E).** Use ⅜"-thick pieces of scrap wood for spacers between the slats to keep them properly aligned during the assembly process.

APPLY THE FINISHING TOUCHES. Fill all open screw holes and voids in the plywood using a quality wood filler. Finish-sand the surfaces and edges of the rocker by hand or with a palm

TIP

When using a router to cut a groove, measure the distance from the cutting edge of the router bit to the outside edge of the router base. Set your straightedge this distance from the layout marks on your workpiece to properly cut along the layout lines.

sander, generally up to 150-grit. Be sure to use a quality primer and then a quality enamel paint, designed for exterior use and greater durability. Choose a light color to reduce the heat absorption from direct sunlight.

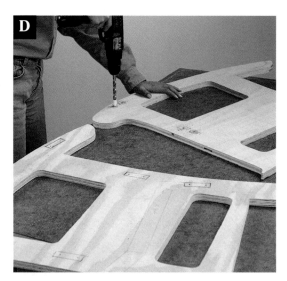

Drill pilot holes to fasten the stretchers to the sides. Counterbore the holes to recess the screw heads.

Fasten the back slats to the stretchers. Use spacers to hold the slats in position during fastening

Hammock Stand

Now you can enjoy the unique pleasure of napping in your own hammock—even if there isn't a tree or fence post in sight.

CONSTRUCTION MATERIALS	
Quantity	**Lumber**
3	1 × 8" × 10' pine
1	1 × 8" × 8' pine
6	1 × 10" × 8' pine
1	2 × 4" × 8' pine
2	2 × 8" × 8' pine

For everyone who has longed for the pleasure of having a backyard hammock, but has lacked a good spot to hang one, this hammock stand is a dream come true. With this Adirondack-inspired structure proudly stationed on your patio or deck, you'll be well on your way to forgetting your day-to-day pressures and worries in the smooth, rocking motions of your own private hammock.

This hammock stand is large enough to accommodate even an extra–wide hammock, like the one above. Its wide, sturdy base and firm uprights make it virtually impossible to overturn, even when you're rocking away at full tilt.

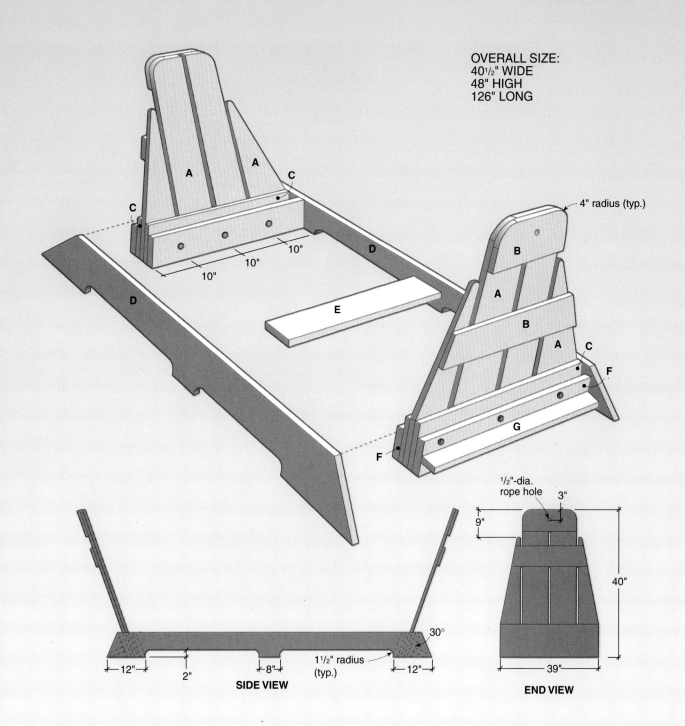

OVERALL SIZE:
40½" WIDE
48" HIGH
126" LONG

4" radius (typ.)

A
A
C
C
B
A
B
A
C
F
D
D
E
G
F

10"
10"
10"
10"

½"-dia.
rope hole
9"
3"
40"
39"

END VIEW

12"
2"
8"
1½" radius
(typ.)
30°
12"

SIDE VIEW

Cutting List

Key	Part	Dimension	Pcs.	Material
A	End panel slat	¾ × 9¼ × 48"	8	Pine
B	Upper cross tie	¾ × 7¼ × 39"	4	Pine
C	Lower cross tie	¾ × 9¼ × 39"	4	Pine
D	Side rail	¾ × 7¼ × 105"	2	Pine

Cutting List

Key	Part	Dimension	Pcs.	Material
E	Stringer	¾ × 7¼ × 39"	1	Pine
F	Standard brace	1½ × 7¼ × 39"	4	Pine
G	Rear brace	1½ × 3½ × 39"	2	Pine

Materials: Deck screws (1¼", 2", 2½"), 6⅜ × 6" carriage bolts with washers and nuts, finishing materials.

Note: Measurements reflect the actual size of dimensional lumber.

Directions:
Hammock Stand

ASSEMBLE THE STANDARDS. The standards are the slat assemblies at the ends of the stand that support the hammock. Our strategy for building them is to join the 1 × 10 slats together, then cut them to shape as if they were one workpiece. First, cut the end panel slats (A) and lower panel cross ties (C) to length from 1 × 10 pine. Cut the upper panel cross ties (B) to length from 1 × 8 pine. Using the cutoff scraps as spacers, lay out the slats on a flat surface to form a 48 × 39" panel with ¾" spacing between the slats. Depending on the actual width of the 1 × 10 material (9¼" is typical), you may have to adjust the spacing between the slats to make the panel 39" wide. Lay one lower panel cross tie across the bottom of the panel, flush with the bottoms of the slats— use a square to make sure the slats are perpendicular to the cross tie. Fasten the lower cross tie to each slat with two 1¼" deck screws. Measure up from the bottom edge of the lower cross tie 20", and mark a line across the slats. Position one upper panel cross tie on the layout line, and the other flush with the top ends of the slats. Fasten the slats to the cross ties with deck screws. Attach slats to cross ties to make 39 × 48" panels for both standards.

TIP

If you already own a hammock that you wish to use, take measurements before building a stand. Adjust the dimensions of the stand, if necessary, to fit your hammock. The hammock stand shown here will hold even large hammocks with crosspieces up to 4' wide and 7' apart. The distance between the tops of the standards should be at least 3' longer than the space between hammock crosspieces.

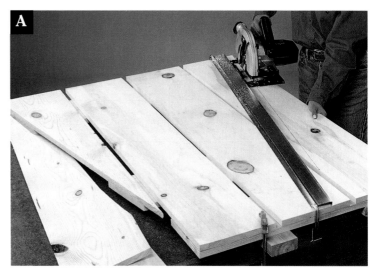

Cut the end panel taper using a straight-line cutting jig and circular saw. Be sure to stop the cut at the inside slats.

Drive additional 2" screws from the front and back to draw the lower cross-ties tightly against the slats that make up the standards.

CUT & SHAPE THE STANDARDS. On the side of one panel that has no cross ties attached, measure down 9" on the inside edge of each outer slat and place a mark. Draw straight lines connecting each mark with the point where the top of the lower cross tie meets the outside edge of each outer slat. Cut along this line with a circular saw and straightedge **(photo A),** cutting through the cross ties as well as the end panel slats. Make similar cuts on both edges of both stan-

dards. Also cut roundovers at the top corners of the standards (see page 83) with a jig saw, then sand smooth with a belt sander and medium-grit (#100 to 120) sandpaper. Smooth out the pointed tips of the outer slats, then turn the standards over and attach lower cross ties, flush with the bottom edges of the standards. For extra strength, drive a few 2" deck screws through each cross-tie to draw the cross ties together **(photo B).**

MAKE THE SIDE RAILS & BRACE COMPONENTS. Cut the side rails (D) to length from 1 × 8 lumber. Measure in from each top end 5¼", and draw cutting lines that connect with the corner at the opposite edge. Cut along the lines with a circular saw **(photo C).** To create feet in the side rails, lay out and cut a pair of 2"-deep cutouts in the bottoms of the rails (see page 83). Cut the stringer (E) to size from 1 × 8 lumber; cut the standard braces (F) from 2 × 8 lumber; and cut the rear braces (G) from 2 × 4 lumber.

ASSEMBLE THE HAMMOCK STAND. At the ends of the side rails, draw 30° reference lines pointing in the opposite direction from the 30° bevels at the ends of the rails. Use the reference lines as guides for attaching the standard braces at a 30° angle between the side rails at each end of the hammock stand (see page 83). Use 2" deck screws and glue to attach the standard braces. Attach the rear braces behind the standard braces for extra support. Then, set a pair of 2¼" spacers against the inside face of each standard brace, and use them to set the gap for installing the inner standard braces **(photo D).** The standards are inserted between the standard braces. Install inner standard braces at both ends of the side rails. Position the stringer at the midpoint of the side rails, 3" down from the top edges, and attach with 2" deck screws. Set the standards into the standard brace slots at each end of the assembly. Drill three evenly spaced ⅜"-dia. holes through each standard/standard brace assembly, about 1" down from the tops of the braces. Insert

6"-long carriage bolts and secure with washers and nuts to hold the standards in place.

APPLY THE FINISHING TOUCHES. Measure down 3" from the top of each standard, and mark a drilling point on each upper cross tie, between the two middle slats. Drill a ½"-dia. hole for the hammock rope at each point.

Sand all edges and surfaces, and apply finish. We used light wood stain and water-based polyurethane (exterior-rated). Hang your hammock in the

stand by threading the cords through the holes in the standards and tying a doubled square knot at the end of the rope. Pull the rope as taut as you can before tying the knot—hammocks will sag when put to use.

Mark points 5¼" in from each side-rail end, then draw cutting lines between the points and the corner on the opposite edge of the rail.

Attach outer cross ties at a 30° angle, then attach the back cleats. Insert 2¼" spacers to set the gap between outer and inner cross ties.

Grill Garage

Eliminate mess and clutter and shelter grilling appliances from the elements with this spacious grill garage.

CONSTRUCTION MATERIALS	
Quantity	**Lumber**
2	⁷⁄₁₆" × 4 × 8' textured cedar sheet siding
1	¾" × 2 × 2' plywood
10	1 × 2" × 8' cedar

Summer cookouts will be more enjoyable with this handy grill garage and storage unit. Unlike most prefabricated grill garages, this project is sized to house today's popular gas grills, as well as traditional charcoal grills, when they are not being used. And while you are using your grill, the spacious top platforms of the grill garage can be used as staging and serving areas for your convenience. The walls of this grill garage are made from inexpensive, attractive rough cedar siding panels. Fitted with a cabinet-style door, the storage compartment can accommodate two large bags of charcoal, plus all your grilling accessories.

OVERALL SIZE:
25 1/2" WIDE
49 3/16" HIGH
62" LONG

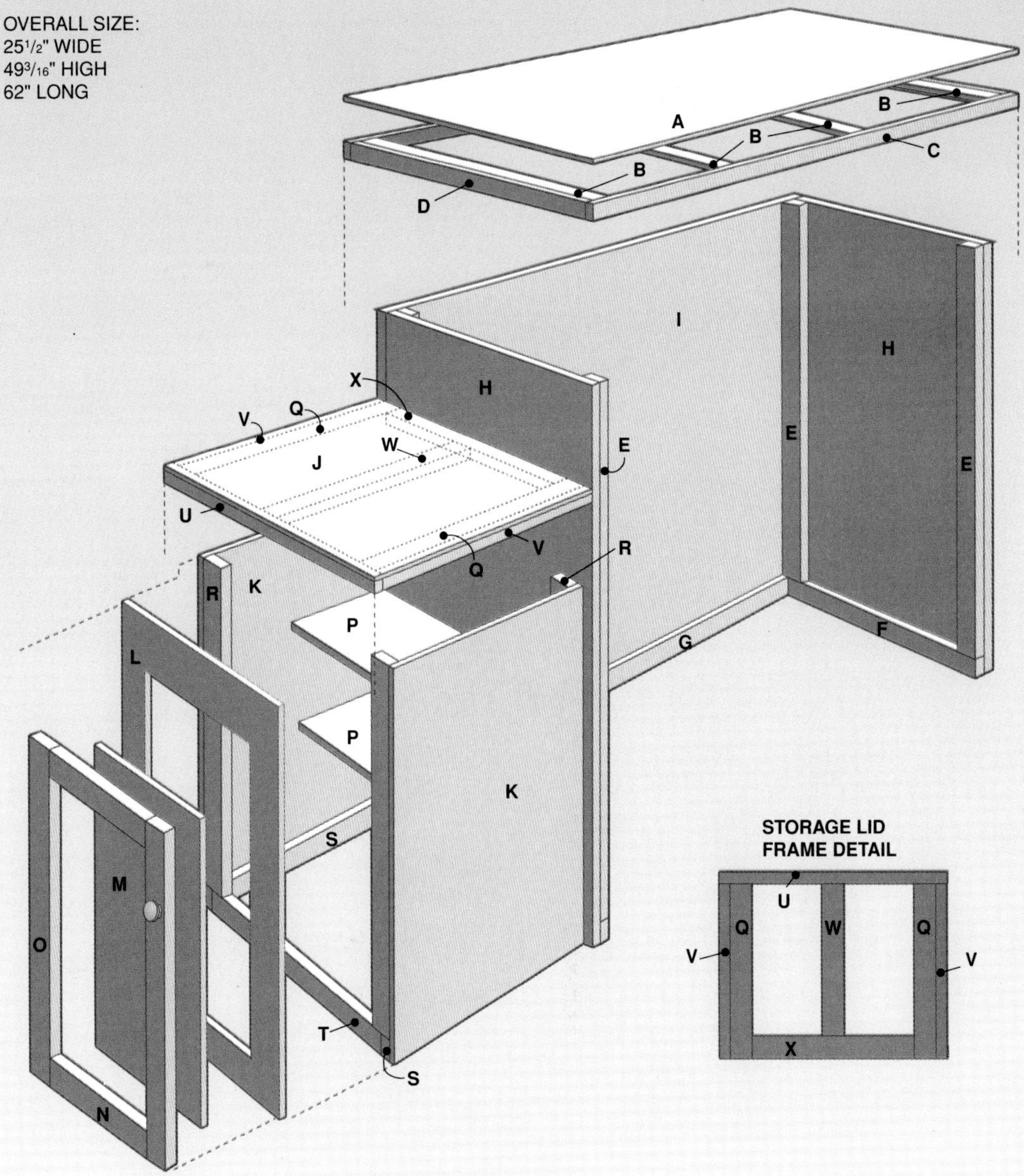

Cutting List

Key	Part	Dimension	Pcs.	Material
A	Garage lid	7/16 × 25 1/2 × 43 5/8"	1	Cedar siding
B	Lid stringer	3/4 × 1 1/2 × 24"	4	Cedar
C	Lid-frame side	3/4 × 1 1/2 × 43 5/8"	2	Cedar
D	Lid-frame end	3/4 × 1 1/2 × 24"	2	Cedar
E	Posts	3/4 × 1 1/2 × 46 1/2"	4	Cedar
F	End plate	3/4 × 1 1/2 × 23 9/16"	2	Cedar
G	Back plate	3/4 × 1 1/2 × 39 3/4"	1	Cedar
H	End panel	7/16 × 24 × 48"	2	Cedar siding
I	Back panel	7/16 × 41 1/4 × 48"	1	Cedar siding
J	Storage lid	7/16 × 20 × 24"	1	Cedar siding
K	Side panel	7/16 × 18 × 29 1/4"	2	Cedar siding
L	Face panel	7/16 × 22 1/2 × 29 1/4"	1	Cedar siding

Cutting List

Key	Part	Dimension	Pcs.	Material
M	Door panel	7/16 × 18 1/2 × 23 1/4"	1	Cedar siding
N	Door rail	3/4 × 1 1/2 × 17"	2	Cedar
O	Door stile	3/4 × 1 1/2 × 24 3/4"	2	Cedar
P	Shelf	3/4 × 10 × 21 5/8"	2	Plywood
Q	End stringer	3/4 × 1 1/2 × 19 1/4"	2	Cedar
R	Short post	3/4 × 1 1/2 × 27 3/4"	4	Cedar
S	Side plate	3/4 × 1 1/2 × 17 1/8"	2	Cedar
T	Front plate	3/4 × 1 1/2 × 20 1/8"	1	Cedar
U	Front lid edge	3/4 × 1 1/2 × 24"	1	Cedar
V	Storage lid end	3/4 × 1 1/2 × 19 1/4"	2	Cedar
W	Center stringer	3/4 × 1 1/2 × 17 3/4"	1	Cedar
X	Rear lid edge	3/4 × 1 1/2 × 19 1/2"	1	Cedar

Materials: Moisture-resistant glue, deck screws (1", 1 1/2", 2", 3"), hinges, door pull, finishing materials.

Note: Measurements reflect actual thickness of dimensional lumber.

Install stringers inside the garage-lid frame to strengthen the garage lid.

Use 1 × 2 posts to create the framework for the main garage compartment.

Directions: Grill Garage

MAKE THE GARAGE LID PANEL. Cut the garage lid (A), to size from a cedar siding panel. Cut the lid stringers (B), lid-frame sides (C) and lid-frame ends (D), to size from 1 × 2 cedar. On a flat worksurface, arrange the frame ends and sides on edge to form the lid frame. Fasten the lid edges and lid ends together with glue and 1½" deck screws driven through the sides and into the ends of the lid-frame ends. Position the lid stringers facedown inside the frame, with one on each end and two spaced evenly between them. Fasten the stringers to the frame with glue and screws **(photo A).** Turn the frame over so the side where the stringers are flush with the top edges of the

frame is facing up. Lay the garage lid on top of the frame assembly and test the fit—the edges of the lid should be flush with the edges of the frame. Remove the garage lid and run a bead of glue on the top edges of the frame. Reposition the lid on the frame assembly and fasten with 1" deck screws driven through counterbored pilot holes in the lid and into the tops of the frame members.

BUILD THE GARAGE WALLS. Cut the posts (E) and end plates (F) to length from 1 × 2 cedar. Cut the end panels (H) to size from textured cedar sheet siding. Use a straightedge cutting guide whenever cutting sheet goods. Assemble an end plate and two posts into an open-end frame on your worksurface, and fasten the parts together with glue and screws driven through the posts and into the ends of the end plate **(photo B).** Test the fit, then attach an end panel to the

frame with glue and counterbored screws **(photo C).** Build the other end panel the same way.

ASSEMBLE THE GARAGE PANELS. Connect the end-panel assemblies with the back panel to create the walls for the main garage compartment. Cut the back plate (G) to length from 1 × 2 cedar, and cut the back panel (I) to size from textured cedar sheet siding. Stand one end-panel assembly up so it rests on the plate, and place a bead of glue along the edge of the post that will join the back panel. Position one end of the back panel flush against the post, making sure the rough side of the cedar siding is facing out. Attach the back panel to the end-panel assembly with 1½" screws. Attach the other end-panel assembly to the other side of the back panel the same way **(photo D).** Place

Attach the end panel to the open-ended frame assembly, making sure that the rough side of the cedar siding is facing outward.

storage-lid end/edge assembly to the end stringer/ rear-lid edge assembly with glue and screws to form a frame. Position the center stringer midway between the end stringers and attach with glue and screws. Turn the storage lid frame over so the side where the stringers are flush with the tops of the frame is facing up. Lay the storage lid panel on top of the frame to make sure the edges are flush, then attach the lid panel with glue and counterbored screws.

BUILD THE CABINET WALLS. Cut the short posts (R) and side plates (S) to length from 1×2 cedar. Then cut the side panels (K) to size from textured cedar sheet siding. Attach a side plate to the bottom, inside edge of a side panel, making sure the plate is flush with the front edge of the panel **(photo E).** Attach a short post upright

a bead of glue along the outside face of the back plate and position the plate at the bottom of the back panel, so the ends of the plate form butt joints with the end-panel assemblies. Secure with 1" screws driven through the back panel and into the back plate. Fit the garage lid panel around the tops of the end and back panels, shifting the panels slightly as needed to create a tight fit. Attach the lid panel with glue and counterbored 2" deck screws driven through the lid frame and into the tops of the end and back panels.

BUILD THE CABINET LID. The cabinet is constructed with an open side that fits against the left end wall of the grill garage. Start by cutting the storage lid (J) to size from textured cedar sheet siding. Cut the end stringers (Q), center stringer (W), front lid edge (U), rear lid edge (X), and storage lid ends (V) to size from 1×2 cedar.

Lay the two storage lid ends and the front lid edge on edge on a flat surface. Position the storage lid ends so that they butt into the back face of the front lid edge. Fasten the ends and edge together with glue and 1½" screws. Lay the rear lid edge on its face between the end stringers, which are facedown, flush with the ends of the stringers. Mounting the rear lid edge in this manner will provide a flush fit at the rear of the storage unit assembly while maintaining an overhang on the sides and front. Fasten the rear lid edge and end stringers together with glue and 3" screws. Fasten the

Attach the back panel to the posts of the end panels to assemble the walls of the main grill garage compartment.

Attach the side plate, with the face against the panel, to the bottom edge of the side panel.

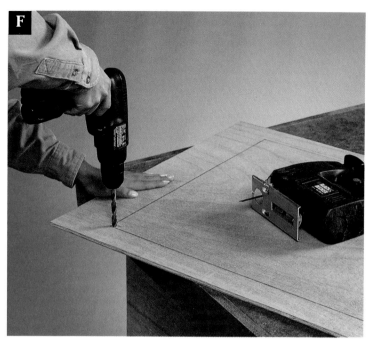

Drill a ³/₈"-dia. hole on the inside of one of the corners of the door layout, then cut out the door opening with a jig saw.

on the end of the side plate that is flush with the side panel, by driving a deck screw up through the plate and into the end of the post. Also drive a screw through the side panel and into the post. This post functions as a cleat for attaching the cabinet to the wall of the garage. Attach another short post in a similar position at the other side of the side panel. Build the second cabinet side panel the same way.

MAKE THE CABINET DOOR FACE FRAME. Cut the face-frame panel (L) from cedar siding. On the inside of the panel, mark a cutout for the cabinet door opening. First, measure down from the top 4", and draw a line across the panel. Then, measure in from both sides 2" and draw straight lines across the panel. Finally, draw a line 2" up from the bottom. The layout lines should form an 18½" × 23¼" rectangle. Drill a

³/₈"-dia. starter hole for a jig saw blade at one corner of the cutout area **(photo F).** Cut out the door opening with a jig saw, then sand the edges smooth. Save the cutout piece: it can be used to make the door panel (M).

ASSEMBLE THE CABINET. Arrange the cabinet walls so they are 24½" apart, then attach the face frame to a short post on each wall, using glue and screws. Make sure the face frame is flush with the outside faces of the cabinet walls, and that the wide "rail" of the face frame is at the top of the cabinet, where there are no plates **(photo G).** Cut the front plate (T) and fasten it to the bottom, inside edge of the face frame, butted against the short posts. Place the cabinet lid assembly onto the cabinet walls and face frame, and attach the cabinet lid with glue and screws driven through the insides of the cabinet walls and into the frame of the lid **(photo H).**

MAKE & INSTALL THE SHELVES. Start by cutting the shelves (P) to size from plywood. Lay out ¾ × 1½" notches in the back corners of the shelves so they fit around the cabinet posts that cleat the top to the garage wall. Cut out the notches in the shelves, using a jig saw. On the inside of each cabinet wall, draw lines 8" down from the top and 11" up from the bottom to mark shelf locations. Fit the shelf notches around the back posts, then attach the shelves by driving deck screws through the cabinet sides and into the edges of the shelves— drive at least two screws into each shelf edge.

ATTACH THE CABINET TO THE GARAGE. Push the cabinet flush against the left wall of the garage. Fasten the cabinet to the garage with deck screws driven through the garage posts and into the short posts of the cabinet. Three screws into each post will provide sufficient holding power.

Fasten the cutout face frame to the cabinet sides.

Set the cabinet-lid assembly over the cabinet walls and face frame, then fasten with glue and screws

Fasten the door rails and door stiles to the door panel using glue and screws, leaving a ¾" overlap on all sides of the door panel.

APPLY THE FINISHING TOUCHES. Sand and smooth out the edges of the grill garage and prepare it for the finish of your choice. Since it is constructed with cedar, we chose a clear wood sealer that does not alter the rich wood grain and color. If you prefer a painted finish, be sure to use a quality primer and durable exterior enamel paint.

BUILD & ATTACH THE DOORS. Cut the door rails (N) and stiles (O) to length from 1 × 2 cedar. Using the cutout from the face frame panel (page 90) for the door panel (M), fasten the rails and stiles to the door panel using glue and screws. Leave a ¾" overlap on all sides

(photo I). Be sure to mount the rails between the stiles, but flush with the stile ends. Attach door hinges 3" from the top and bottom of the one door stile, then mount the door to the face frame. Install the door pull.

TIP

The grill garage is designed as a handy storage center for your grill and supplies, such as charcoal and cooking utensils. Do not store heavy items on top of the garage lid, and never light your grill while it is still in the grill garage. Do not store lighter fluid in the grill garage— always keep lighter fluid out of reach of children in a cool, sheltered area, like a basement.

Party Cart

A fully insulated cooler on wheels, our party cart has some clever bells and whistles, as well as distinctive design elements so it will fit in even at the most formal outdoor gatherings.

CONSTRUCTION MATERIALS

Quantity	Lumber
4	2 × 4" × 8' cedar
2	1 × 4" × 8' cedar
1	1 × 10" × 4' cedar
3	1 × 3" × 8' cedar
1	1 × 2" × 6' cedar
2	4 × 8' ½"-thick BCX plywood
1	4 × 8' sheet tileboard
1	1"-dia. × 3' oak dowel
1	1½" × 4' × 8' foam insulation

Outdoor entertaining events often turn into an endless parade between the patio and the refrigerator, or a loose huddle around an old foam cooler. With this portable party cart, you can keep your guests refreshed on site and in style. The tileboard top is generously proportioned and easy to clean. With a capacity of 15 cubic feet, the insulated cooler compartment has plenty of room for cans, bottles, even kegs, as well as ice and snacks. You can add accessories to help the cart meet your needs. A few suggestions: attach a bottle opener, paper towel holder, or plastic cup dispenser to the cabinet side; drill a 1"-diameter hole through the side to create a passage for a keg hose, then cover the hole with a plastic grommet; mount a flagpole holder on the back of the cart to hold a beach umbrella.

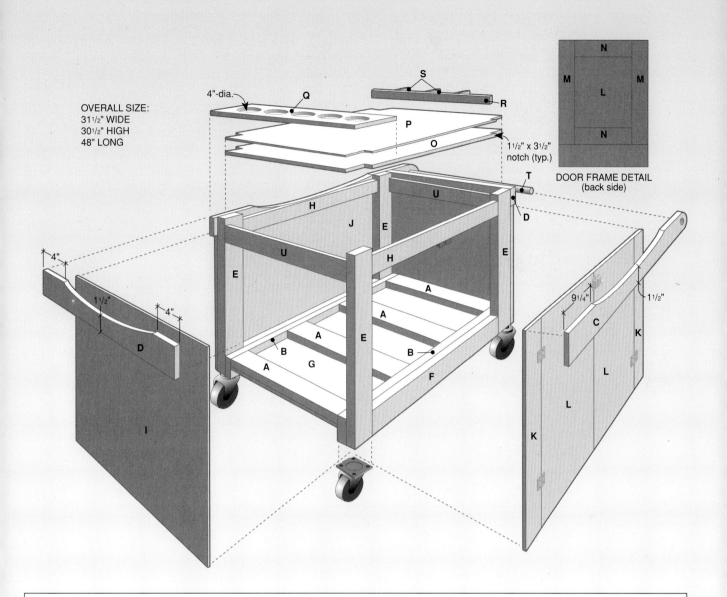

OVERALL SIZE:
31½" WIDE
30½" HIGH
48" LONG

4"-dia.

1½" x 3½" notch (typ.)

DOOR FRAME DETAIL
(back side)

Cutting List				
Key	**Part**	**Dimension**	**Pcs.**	**Material**
A	Bottom stretcher	1½ × 3½ × 24"	4	Cedar
B	Bottom side rail	1½ × 3½ × 42"	2	Cedar
C	Top side rail	⅞ × 3½ × 48"	2	Cedar
D	Top end rail	⅞ × 3½ × 30"	2	Cedar
E	Post	1½ × 3½ × 30"	4	Cedar
F	Rail filler	1½ × 3½ × 35"	2	Cedar
G	Bottom	½ × 24 × 42"	1	BCX plywood
H	Tabletop cleat	⅞ × 2½ × 35"	2	Cedar
I	End panel	½ × 30 × 27"	2	BCX plywood
J	Side panel	½ × 43 × 27"	1	BCX plywood
K	Post cover	½ × 4 × 27"	2	BCX plywood

Cutting List				
Key	**Part**	**Dimension**	**Pcs.**	**Material**
L	Door	½ × 17⅜ × 27"	2	BCX plywood
M	Door stile	⅞ × 2½ × 21⅞"	4	Cedar
N	Door rail	⅞ × 2½ × 10¼"	4	Cedar
O	Tabletop	½ × 30 × 42"	1	BCX plywood
P	Waterproof panel	⅛ × 30 × 42"	2	Tileboard
Q	Bottle caddy	⅞ × 9¼ × 31½"	1	Cedar
R	Bin side	⅞ × 1½ × 30"	1	Cedar
S	Bin divider	⅞ × 1½ × 8¼"	3	Cedar
T	Handle	1"-dia. × 31½"	1	Oak dowel
U	Tabletop end cleat	¾ × 2½ × 27"	2	Cedar

Materials: Deck screws (1", 1½", 2", 2½", 3"), 6d casing nails, (4) 2" brass butt hinges, brass clasp, (2) magnetic door catches, (2) brass window sash handles, (4) heavy-duty locking casters, moisture-resistant glue, tileboard adhesive, panel adhesive, ⅜"-dia. cedar plugs.

Note: Measurements reflect the actual size of dimensional lumber.

Attach the scooped top frame pieces to the posts with 2" deck screws. Posts are attached to the base frame with 3" deck screws.

Attach the plywood cabinet sides and the cabinet base to the cabinet frame with 1¼" deck screws

Directions: Party cart

BUILD THE CABINET FRAME. The main structural element of our party cart is a cabinet frame made from 2 × 4 and 1 × 4 cedar. Start by cutting the bottom stretchers (A) and bottom side rails (B) from 2 × 4s. Lay the rails on edge on your worksurface, then set the stretchers facedown between the rails. One stretcher should be set flush at each end, with the other two spaced evenly between the ends (the assembly should look like a ladder). Drill pilot holes, then fasten the side rails to the stretchers with 3" deck screws. Then, cut the top side rails (C) and top end rails (D) from 1 × 4s. Cut a gentle, 1½"-deep scoop into each top rail, using your jig saw. The scoops should start 4" from each end of the top end rails. In the top side rails, start cutting the scoops 9¼" from the front ends, and 11¼" from the back ends. Assemble the top side and top end rails into a

square frame. The back end rail should be recessed 6" from the back ends of the side rails. Drill pilot holes with ⅜"-dia. × ¼"-deep counterbores through the side rails and into the end rails. Fasten the rails together with glue and 2" deck screws, then plug the counterbores with ⅜"-dia. cedar plugs. Cut the 2 × 4 posts (E), and arrange them so they fit at the outside corners of the 2 × 4 frame base and the inside corners of the 1 × 4 frame top. Make sure the frame base is positioned with the recesses beneath the stretchers facing down. Attach the top and bottom frames to the posts with 3" deck screws and glue at the bottom, and 2" deck screws and glue at the top **(photo A).**

ATTACH SIDE PANELS TO CABI-NET FRAME. To form the cabinet for the cooler compartment, wrap the cabinet frame with plywood. Before you attach the plywood, attach a 2 × 4 rail filler (F) to the outer face of each bottom side rail in the

frame base. The rail fillers eliminate gaps between the side rails and the sides of the cabinet. Cut the rail fillers, then attach them to the bottom side rails with 2½" deck screws. Cut the bottom panel (G) from ½"-thick plywood and attach it to the underside of the frame base with 1½" deck screws. The top panel rests on cleats fastened to the inside faces of the 1 × 4s at the top of the cabinet frame. Measure down 2¼" from the tops of the frame pieces, then draw reference lines for the cleats. Cut the 1 × 3 table-top cleats (H) and attach them just below the reference lines, using 1½" deck screws. Cut the end panels (I) and the side panel (J) from plywood, and position them against the cabinet frame so all panels overhang the frame base by ½". Attach the panels to the frame with 1" deck screws **(photo B).** Cut post covers (K) from ½" plywood and attach them to the 2 × 4 posts at the open side.

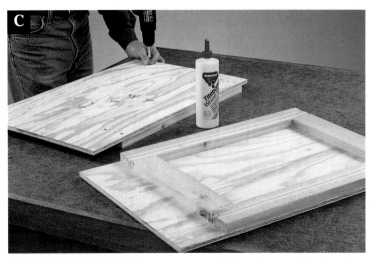

Attach the 1 × 3 door rails and stiles by driving 1" screws through the front faces of the plywood door panels.

Bond tileboard to the plywood tabletop with tileboard adhesive.

BUILD THE DOORS. The cooler compartment doors are made from ½" plywood, with 1 × 3 rails and stiles attached to the back side to stiffen the plywood. Cut the door panels (L), door stiles (M), and door rails (N). Attach the door rails and stiles with glue and 1" screws driven through the fronts of the door panels **(photo C);** attach the upper door rail to the inside (unsanded) edge of each door panel, 1⅝" down from the top edge and centered side to side; attach the lower rail 4¼" up from the bottom of the panel; attach vertical stiles so they are flush with the outer edges of the rails to complete the doors.

BUILD AND INSTALL THE CART TOP. The cart top is cut from ½" plywood, then covered with tileboard to create a smooth, water-resistant surface that is easy to clean. Cut the plywood tabletop panel (O), then cut a piece of ¼"-thick tileboard (P) to the same size. Tileboard is usually sold in 4 × 8' sheets that resemble interior paneling. It is available in a wide variety of textures and finishes. We chose a fairly neutral, biscuit-colored style. If you are willing to spend the extra money, you can sub-

stitute fiberglass shower liner panels for a more long-lasting tabletop surface. Attach the tileboard to the sanded side of the top panel with exterior-rated tileboard adhesive **(photo D),** according to the recommended application methods and drying times. After the adhesive has set, use a jig saw to cut out 1½ × 3½" notches from the corners of the cart top to fit around the cabinet-frame posts. Make sure the cutouts are oriented correctly. Apply a thick bead of panel adhesive to the tops of the 1 × 3 cleats mounted on the inside faces of the frame top, then set the cart top onto the cleats and press down firmly. Do not nail or screw the top in place. Set some heavy weights on the surface while the adhesive dries.

LINE THE COOLER COMPARTMENT. We used 1½"-thick open-cell foam insulation boards to insulate the cooler compartment. For greater durability and better insulation performance, you can substitute closed-cell insulation boards with a puncture-resistant facing. The insulation boards are attached to the interior walls of the cabinet, and to the back sides of the doors, with panel adhesive. Cut insulation boards slightly oversize so you can use compression to help hold them in place. Use a sharp utility knife to cut insulation boards to fit into the gaps between the stretchers on the floor of the cabinet, and to fit between the rails and stiles on the doors. Also cut insula-

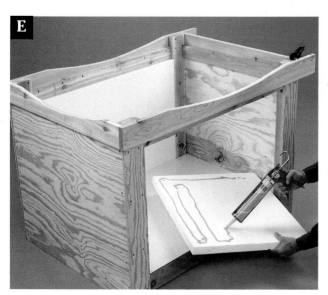

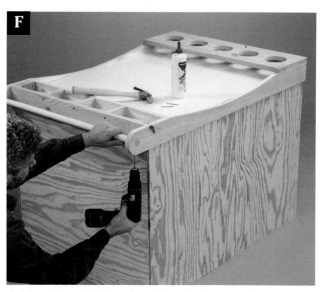

Use panel adhesive to install rigid foam insulation on the interior walls of the cooler compartment.

A 6d casing nail driven through a pilot hole in the frame rail and into each dowel end holds the cart handle in position.

tion to fit the walls and top of the compartment. Attach all the insulation boards **(photo E).** Cut a second piece of tileboard (P) the same size as the top panel. Apply tileboard adhesive to the tops of the exposed stretchers in the frame bottom, and install the tileboard to make a bottom for the compartment. To protect the inside walls and top of the compartment, cut tileboard to fit and attach it to the insulation boards with panel adhesive (optional).

HANG THE DOORS. Center the doors over the door opening, with the top edges aligned, and hang them from the plywood post covers (K) with 2" brass butt hinges. Leave a gap of about ⅛" between doors.

ACCESSORIZE THE TOP. The bottle caddy and napkin/condiment bin are optional features that give the party cart greater versatility. Cut the bottle caddy (Q) from 1 × 10 cedar, then cut evenly spaced 4"-dia. holes in the board. Smooth out the cuts

with a drum sander mounted on your electric drill. Set the bottle caddy over the frame top at the front end of the cart, and attach it to the frame with 1" screws. Cut the bin side (S) and the bin dividers (T) from 1 × 2 cedar. Space the dividers evenly along the divider side, and attach with 1" deck screws. Apply panel adhesive to the bottoms of the dividers and divider side, then set the assembly on the tabletop, with the free ends of the dividers flush against the back rail. Secure the rail to the dividers with 1" screws.

INSTALL THE HANDLE. We used a 1"-dia. oak dowel to make the handle that is mounted between the top frame rails at the back of the cart. Cut the handle (V) to length, then measure in 1" from the back ends of the top frame rails, and mark a point that is centered top-to-bottom. Use this point as a centerpoint to drill 1"-diameter holes through the rails, using a spade bit, to accommodate the handle. For added visual appeal, we used a jig saw to

round off the ends of the rails once our handle position was established. Insert the handle through both 1" holes, so the ends are flush with the outside faces of the rails. Secure the handle by drilling ⅛" pilot holes through the rails and into the ends of the handle, then driving a 6d casing nail into each pilot end of the handle.

FINISH THE CART. We used a clear finish on the exposed cedar trim, then painted the plywood surfaces with exterior-grade enamel paint. Before applying paint and stain, fill exposed plywood edges and nails holes with wood putty, then sand smooth. Sand surface to at least 120-grit. After painting and finishing, install the remaining hardware. To keep the doors closed securely, we used a brass clasp and magnetic door catches. We used brass window sash handles for the door pulls. Because the cart is designed to carry a load in excess of 100 pounds, we installed heavy-duty, locking casters to the bottom of each post.